MEL BAY'S COMPLETE JAZZ TRUMPET BOOK

By William Bay

I0809703

WWW.MELBAY.COM

Contents

Jazz Trumpet Studies

This section was written in order to help the trumpet player read and interpret jazz music. The text begins with basic rhythmic phrasing pertinent to a variety of styles of jazz music. Examples range from Swing Era through Be-Bop and Contemporary Rock/ Jazz. A section is included on special effects such as the shake, gliss, lip trill, etc. Finally, studies are included on playing and learning to hear various chords as a prelude to improvisation.

Remember! While we need to develop and expand our rhythmic and melodic concepts, create our own unique style, and increase our technical ability to execute our ideas, we must continually nurture and train our ear.

Bill Bay

Phrase #1

Basic Rhythmic Concepts for Jazz and Contemporary Phrasing

Phrase #2

This phrase has an alternate interpretation found in some rock and Latin music. We will cover that later.

Easin' On

Mixed Bag

Up tempo

M.J.

Slow groove

Go!

Medium ride

Phrase #3

'Tis Diz

Phrase #4

Blues Riff

Phrase #5

Keep 'Em Short

Phrase #6

Easy Groovin'

Phrase #7

Smooth, legato tonguing is essential for much of jazz music. Ballads especially utilize this phrasing.

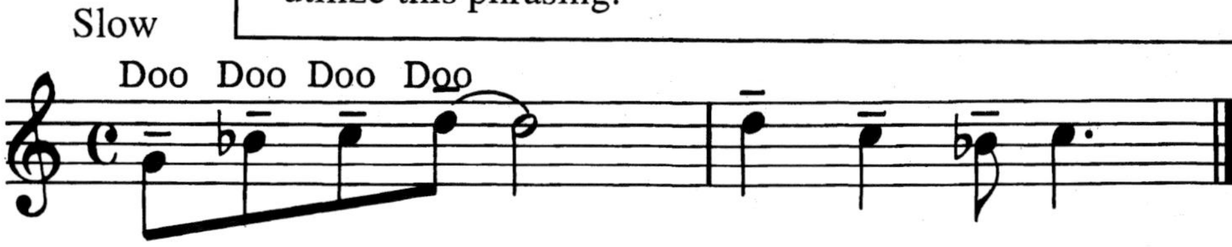

"Smooth-Doo-Tonguing"

Phrase #8

"Slow-Doo-Dot"

Starlight Sounds

Harmon mute-stem removed

Phrase #9

"Swing Riff"

Freddie's Jump

Phrase #10

Big Band Bash

Phrase #11

Opus 11

Phrase #12

Jersey Stomp

Fast

Phrase #13

Soft Winds

Medium
Cup Mute

Phrase #14

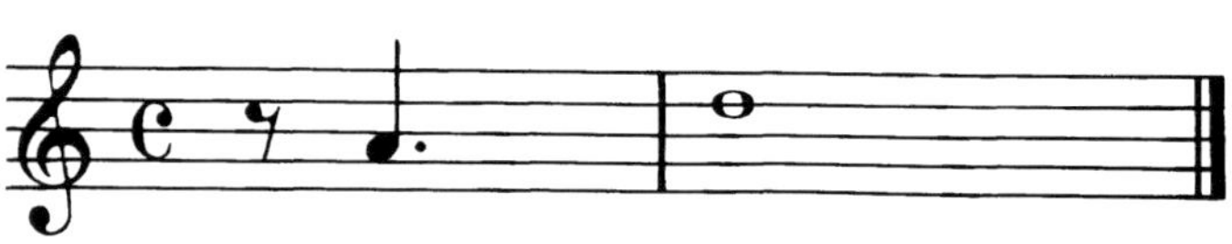

"Kicker"

Medium

Phrase #15

"3/4 Jazz"

Walkin'

Fast-In one

Phrase #16

"Da-Dit-Da-Dit"

Mixed Phrases

Blue Vibes

Revival Blues

Bossa Nova Style
"To Carlos"

Rio

Basie Style
Easy Blowin'

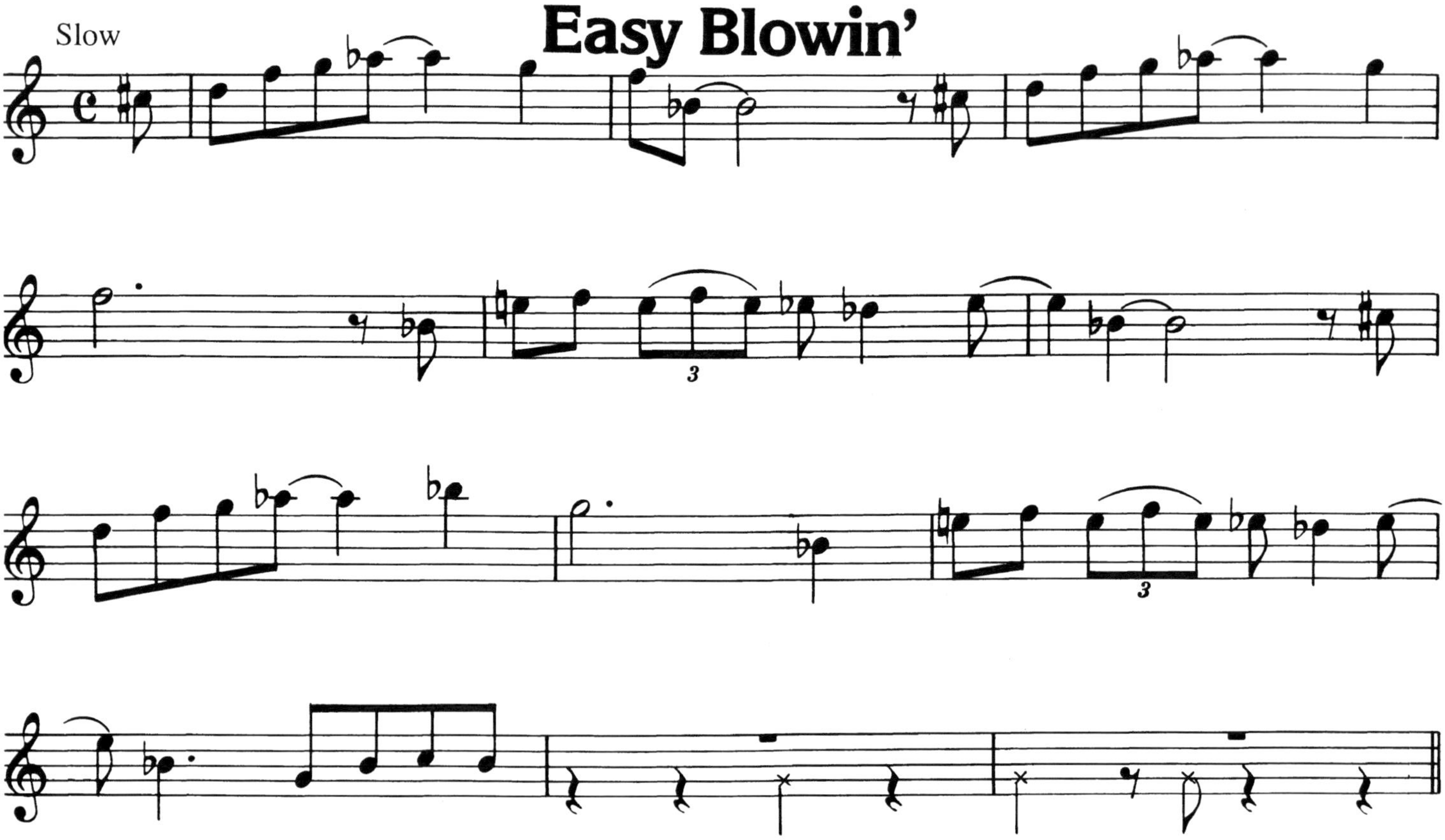

Octave Blues

Special Effects

The Standardization of Stage Band Articulations

HEAVY ACCENT
Hold full value.

HEAVY ACCENT
Hold less than full value.

HEAVY ACCENT
Short as possible.

STACCATO
Short – not heavy.

LEGATO TONGUE
Hold full value.

THE SHAKE
A variation of the tone upwards – much like a trill.

LIP TRILL Similar to shake but slower and with more lip control.

WIDE LIP TRILL Same as above except slower and with wider interval.

THE FLIP Sound note, raise pitch, drop into following note (done with lip on brass)

THE SMEAR Slide into note from below and reach correct pitch just before next note. Do not rob preceding note.

THE DOIT Sound note then gliss upwards from one to five steps.

DU
False or muffled tone

WAH
Full tone – not muffled.

SHORT GLISS UP Slide into* note from below (usually one to three steps).

LONG GLISS UP
Same as above except longer entrance.

SHORT GLISS DOWN The reverse of the short gliss up.

LONG GLISS DOWN Same as long gliss up in reverse.

SHORT LIFT Enter note via chromatic or diatonic scale beginning about a third below.

LONG LIFT
Same as above except longer entrance.

SHORT SPILL Rapid diatonic or chromatic drop. The reverse of the short lift.

LONG SPILL Same as above except longer exit.

THE PLOP A rapid slide down harmonic or diatonic scale before sounding note.

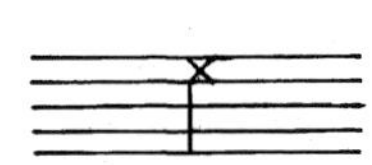
INDEFINITE SOUND
Deadened tone – indefinite pitch.

* NOTE: No individual notes are heard when executing a gliss.

Used by permission from the National Association of Jazz Educators

Heavy Accent #1

(Hold Full Value)

Up tempo

Heavy Accent #2

(Hold Less Than Full Value)

Very fast

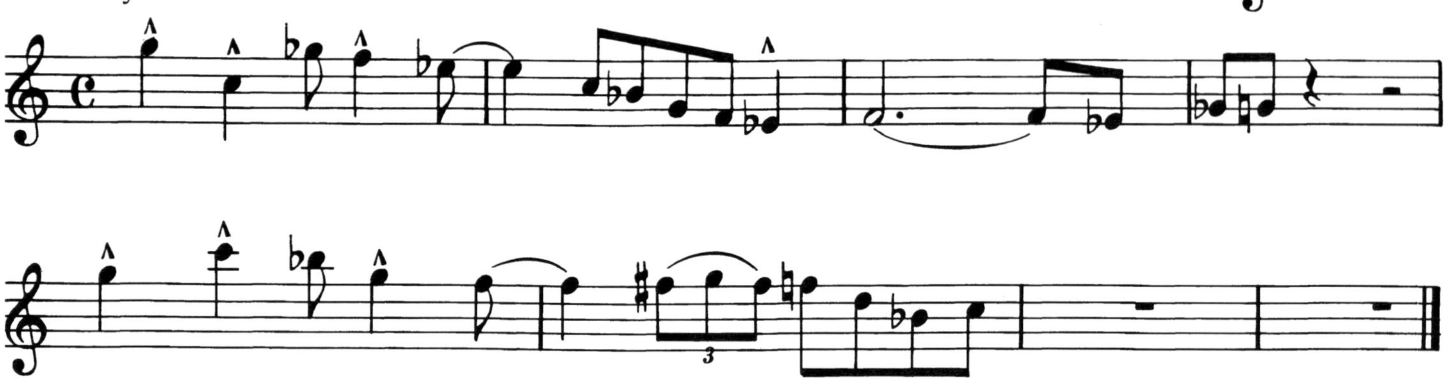

Heavy Accent #3

(Short As Possible)

Up tempo

Standard Staccato 

Latin-Type
Rhumba tempo

Standard Legato 

Bossa Nova tempo

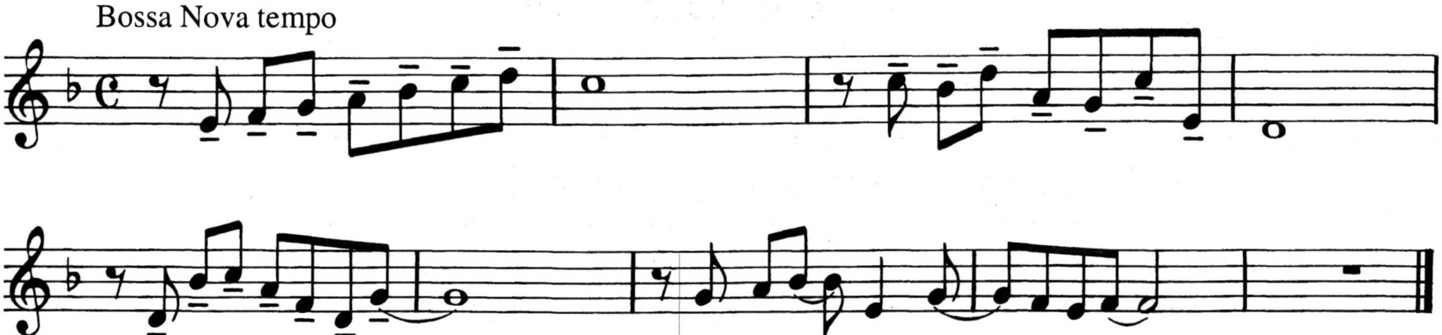

The Shake 

Practice this technique on G (use 1st and 3rd valves) until you gain a degree of control over it. The shake is done primarily by movement of the right hand back and forth.

Up tempo

Lip Trill

This is similar in sound to the shake. However, it usually is slower and, unlike the shake, is performed by the lip.

Wide Lip Trill

Slow, dirty lip trill done with the lips and ranging between the intervals marked.

The Flip

written

sounds like

Fast tempo

The Smear

Press valves 1/2 way down and "slide" into note from lower pitch, or attack note low in pitch and, with the lip, slide into correct pitch.

Slow ballad

The Doit

Play note, press valves 1/2 way down and "slide" up, usually a fifth.

Slow blues

Du-Wah

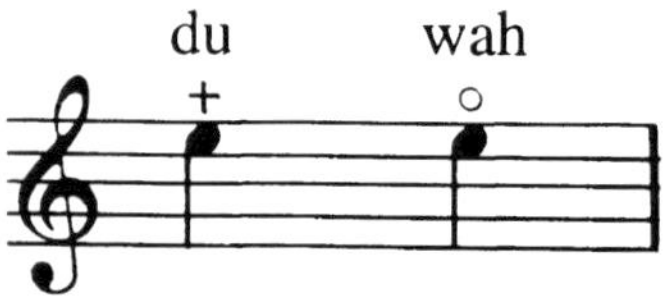

There are basically 2 techniques for muffling the tone. One is to press the valves 1/2 way down on the "du" (+) and to finger the following note on the "wah" (°). The other technique is to place your hand or a plunger mute over the end of the horn on the (+) and to play the horn open on the (°). Practice the following study using both techniques.

Medium tempo

Up Gliss

Clean slide

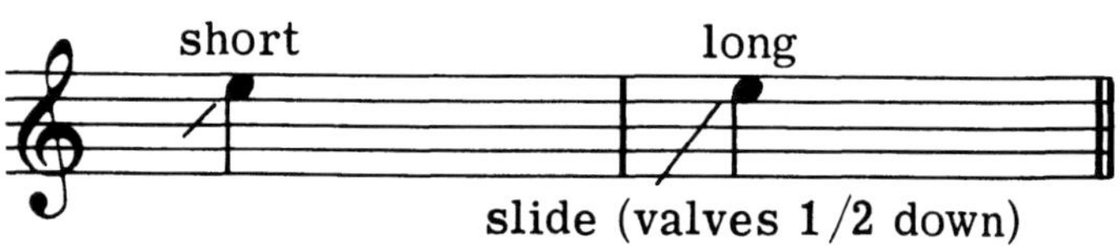

"Rip"

A straight line means to slide into a note (like a trombone slide). A broken or wavy line means to "rip" into a note in such a manner that the individual notes may be heard "ripping" up into the desired pitch.

Slow ballad

Down Gliss

1/2 Value Slide

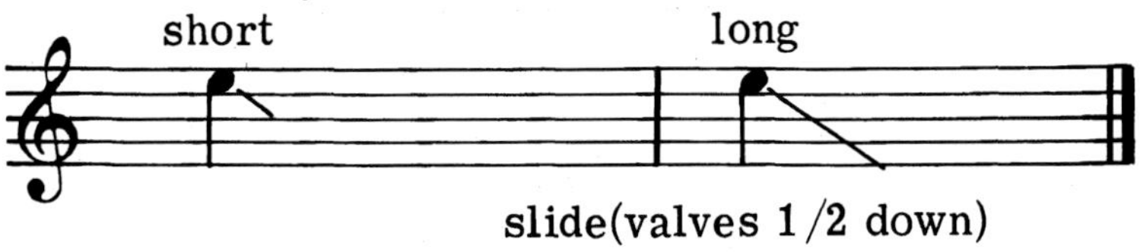

A straight line means to slide down from a note (1/2 valve). A broken line means to fall off a note with the lip so that other notes may be heard while you are "falling off."

Down Rip or Falling Off

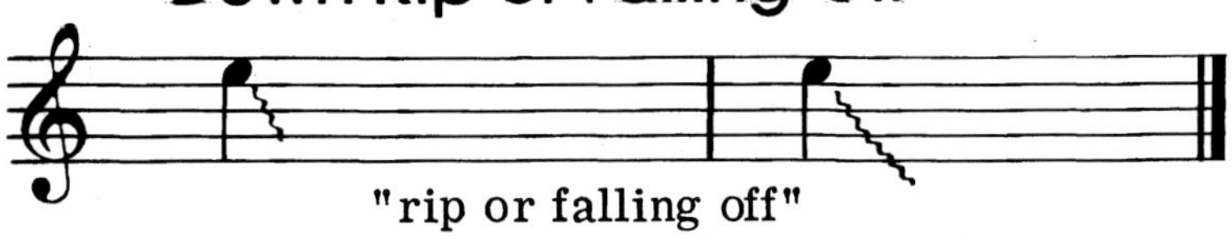

Basie-style blues

Lifts

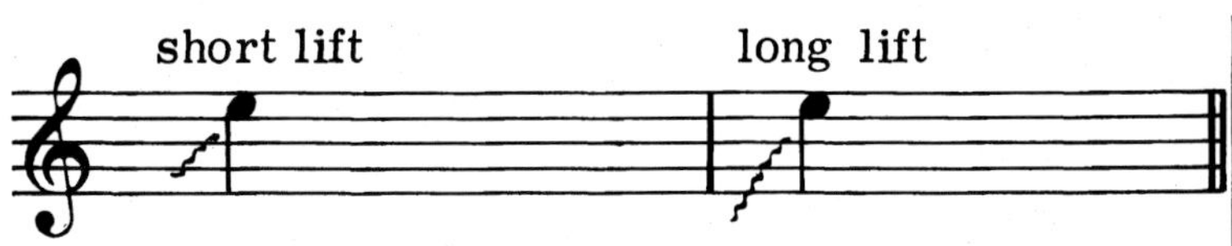

A lift is a technique whereby a trumpet player slurs chromatically or diatonically up to the desired note.

Medium tempo

Spills

The spill is the same technique as the lift, except the trumpet player descends down from a note.

Up tempo

Plop

* I like to describe the plop as a sudden lip drop from a high note to a lower one.

Fast tempo

Indefinite Sound

Usually done by pressing valves 1/2 way down. A muffled sound may also result from numerous lip and tongue variances.

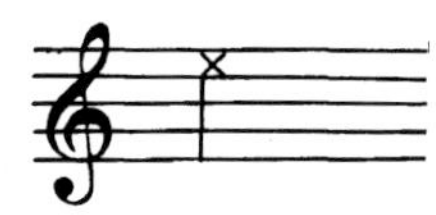

Variances medium

Indefinite Blues

Easy groove

Assorted Techniques

Slow blues

Be-Bop

Much of today's jazz remains under the dominant influence of "be-bop" phrasing. All of the following studies should be played slowly at first. Keep the tonguing light. Remember, the studies should swing. They should not sound mechanical.

Changes

Up tempo

Riff for Clifford

Very fast

Breezin'

Be-Bop Blue

Theme For Bird

Medium

The Messenger

Up tempo

Cookin'

Cool Affair

Rock music is characterized by the hard-driving, straight up-and-down rhythm. Before we start playing contemporary rock and soul-type studies, we need to practice the following studies for phrasing.

Rock

Rhythm

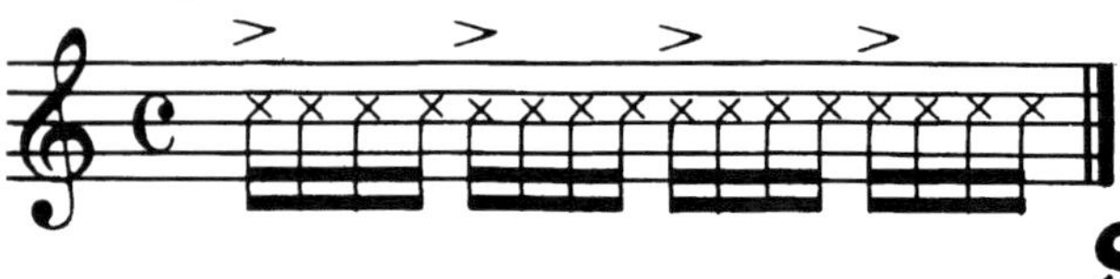

Study #1

Play straight - Rock, not swing feeling

Study #2

Slow rock

Rhythm

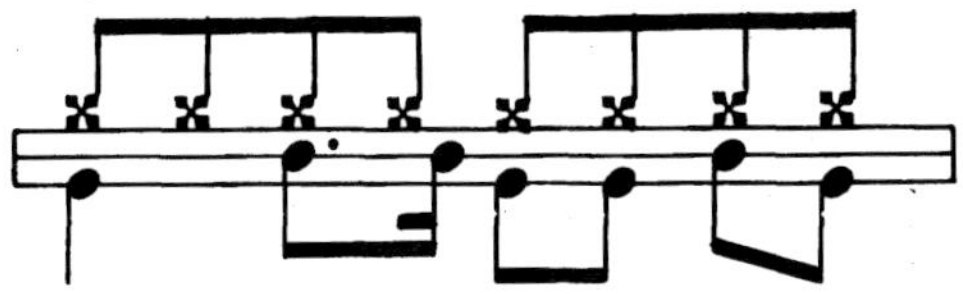

Study #3

Soul Riff

Double time feeling

Soul Groove

Rhythm

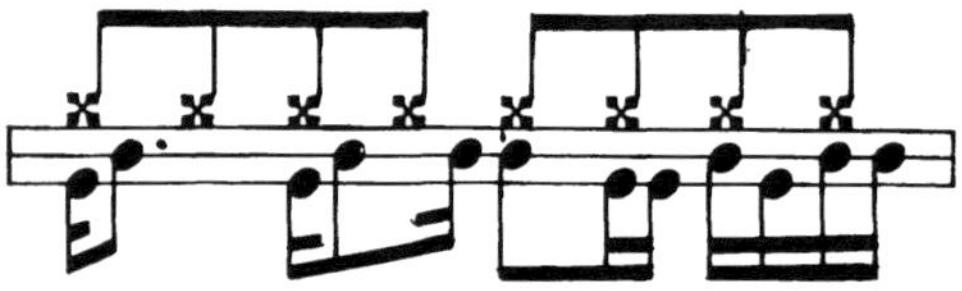

Midnight Ride

Soul Prelude

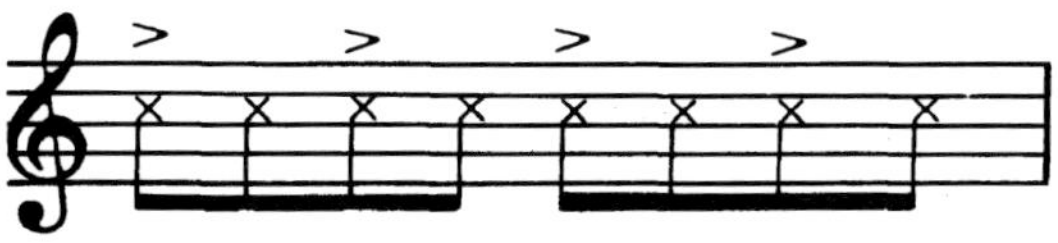

Rhythm

Hard Driver

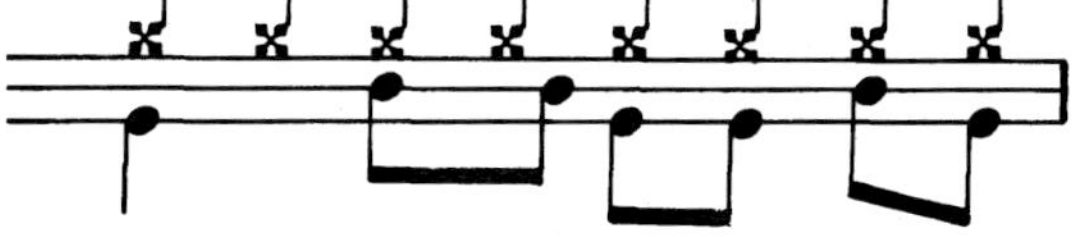

Rhythm

Blues Riff

Rhythm

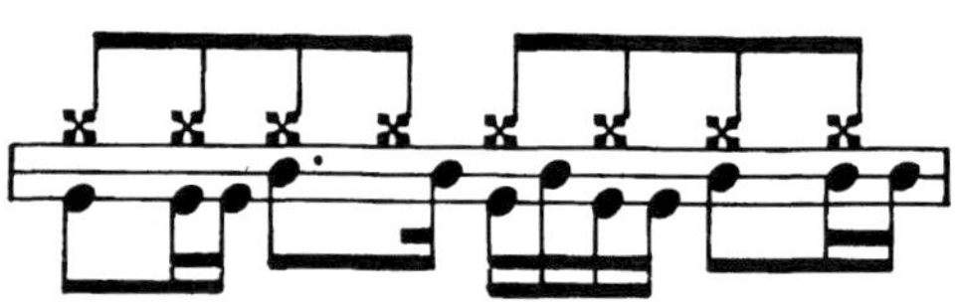

Motown Groove

Choctaw Bridge

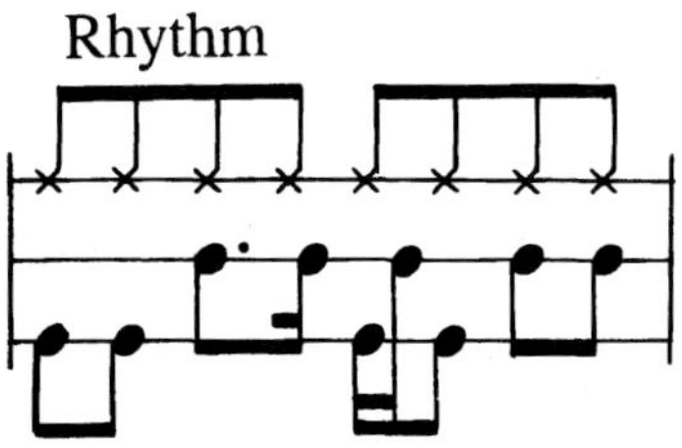

Aretha

Basically Soul

Rhythm

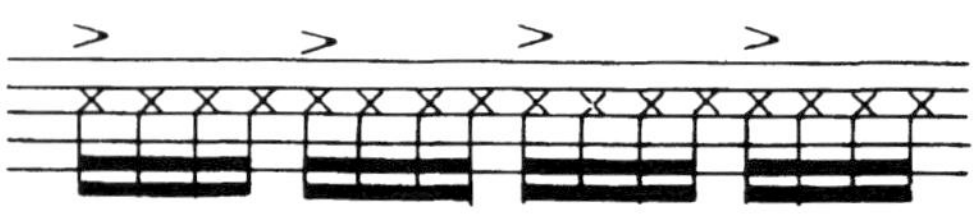

Very fast

Chicago

Up tempo

Latin Rock

Cow Bell

West Side Slide

Medium

Boogie

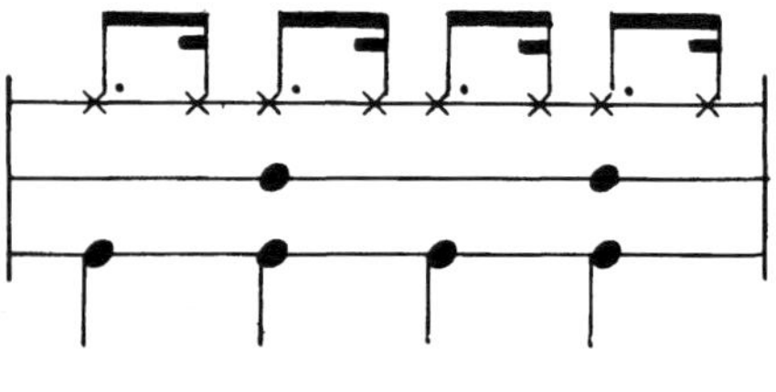

Folk Blues

Jazz Techniques

Jazz and contemporary music require certain techniques (especially in solo performance) which frequently are not perfected in studying traditional trumpet literature. To give an example, crisp and accurate fingering are needed–yet fingering must be done in a manner that "swings." There are two extremes to avoid. I have heard players with great ideas who simply did not have the technique to express themselves properly. Also, I have listened to players with great technique who played so cleanly and "legitimately" that they sounded dated and square. In studying the following pages, remember to achieve sharp and clean technique; but keep in mind that in applying technical facility—you must phrase properly so as to convey the feeling and beat of the music. Remember this—great technique is an incomparable asset to any style.

Basic Finger Calisthenics

Repeat 7 times. Make the fingers "snap." Try to play each exercise in 1 breath.

Movable Patterns

Rhythmic Variations on Pattern #1

Learning to start each of these finger patterns on different beats will be of tremendous help when improvising.

var 1

continue up chromatically

var 2

continue

var 3

continue

var 4

continue

var 5

continue

var 6

continue

var 7

continue

var 8

continue

var 9

continue

var 10

continue

Movable Pattern #2

Variations on Pattern #2

Articulation

The following patterns are valuable as articulation studies and as helpful phrases for playing through chord changes when improvising. First – learn the phrase and be able to "swing" on it. Second – memorize the phrase. Third – play the phrase down or up chromatically. (Playing it up or down through the various keys by **ear** or memory is strongly recommended.) Finally – play the variations on the pattern in all keys by **ear**.

Pattern 1

Variations on Pattern #1

var 1

continue down chromatically

var 2

continue

var 3

continue

var 4

continue

var 5

continue

var 6

continue

var 7

continue

var 8

continue

var 9

continue

Pattern #2

Articulation Variations on Pattern #2

Pattern #3

Articulation Variations on Pattern #3

Chord and Scale Studies

In this section, effort should be made to develop both technical and aural (hearing) skills.

Jazz musicians speak of players who have "good ears." This refers to players who have developed their aural skills to the point where they can instantly recognize and react to scales, chords, and intervals which are either played by someone else or that occur in a player's own mind as an "idea."

To help develop these skills, it is recommended that the student play and sing all of the exercises in this section. The singing is very important as it will help develop the aural skills internally.

Here is a procedure for practicing in this fashion:

1. Play the exercise until it sounds familiar. Really listen to what is being played. Don't ever practice with your "ears closed".
2. Sing the exercise using either syllables, letter names, or scale step numbers.
3. Play it again on the instrument and compare.

The development of these skills is not easy and will probably not come quickly, but serious effort will pay off; and the results are definitely worth the effort.

Chord Studies

The important thing in studying chords is to learn to hear the relationship of intervals within a given chord. Training the ear by applying the following studies will help the clarinet player begin to improvise with both technical and harmonic freedom.

Scale Building

Study the following section on scale building and constructing chords from scale degrees, so that you will understand the musical theory behind the studies that follow.

Major Scale

A major scale is a series of eight notes arranged in a pattern of whole steps and half steps.

C Major Scale

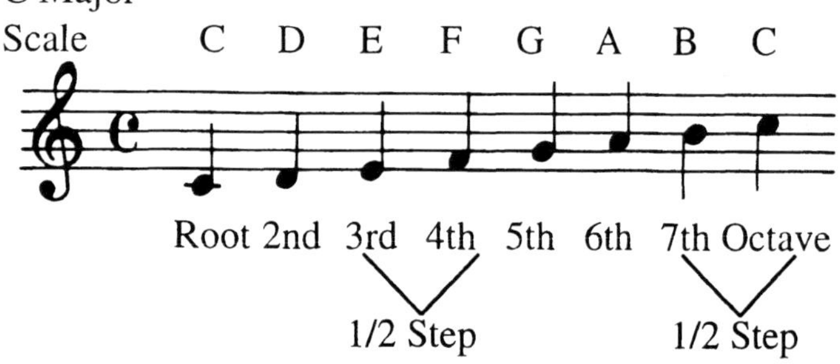

C to D	=	Whole Step
D to E	=	Whole Step
E to F	=	1/2 Step
F to G	=	Whole Step
G to A	=	Whole Step
A to B	=	Whole Step
B to C	=	1/2 Step

To construct a major scale we first start with the name of the scale (frequently called the Root or Tonic). With the C scale this would be the note "C". The rest of the scale would fall in line as follows.

Scale Tones		Distance From Preceding Note
Root	(C)	
2nd	(D)	Whole Step
3rd	(E)	Whole Step
4th	(F)	1/2 Step
5th	(G)	Whole Step
6th	(A)	Whole Step
7th	(B)	Whole Step
Octave	(C)	1/2 Step

With the above formula you can construct any major scale!

G Major Scale

To construct the G major scale, start with the note G, construct it as follows:

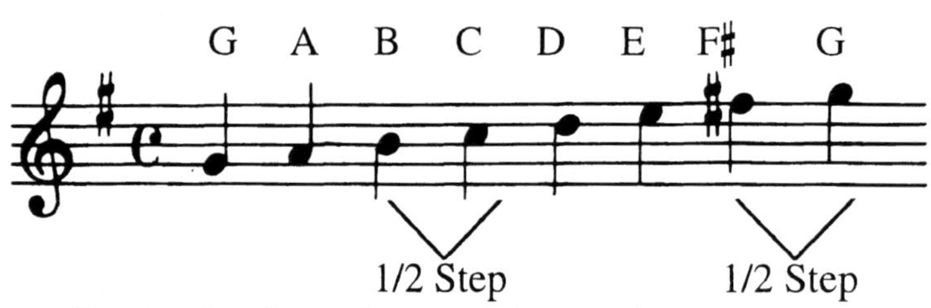

Notice that in order to make our formula work with the G scale we must sharp(♯) the F. There must be a whole step between the 6th and the 7th tones of the scale. In order to establish a whole step between E and F we must sharp the F.

Note: The student's success in learning to hear chords in this section is entirely dependent upon his diligence in playing the chord study examples in all keys!

CHORD BUILDING CHART*

Chord type	Scale Degrees Used	Symbols
Major	Root, 3rd, 5th	Maj
Minor	Root, ♭3rd, 5th	mi,—, m
Diminished	Root, ♭3rd, ♭5th, ♭♭7th	dim,°
Augmented	Root, 3rd, ♯5th	+, aug.
Dominant Seventh	Root, 3rd, 5th, ♭7th	dom, 7, 7
Minor Seventh	Root, ♭3rd, 5th, ♭7th	-7, min7
Major Seventh	Root, 3rd, 5th, maj. 7th	M7, ma7
Major Sixth	Root, 3rd, 5th, 6th	M6, M6, 6
Minor Sixth	Root, ♭3rd, 5th, 6th	mi 6, -6
Seventh ♯5th	Root, 3rd, ♯5th, ♭7th	7^{+5}, $7^{\sharp 5}$
Seventh ♭5th	Root, 3rd, ♭5th, ♭7th	7^{-5}, $7^{\flat 5}$
Major 7th ♭3rd	Root, ♭3rd, 5th, maj. 7th	Ma 7^{-3}
Minor 7th ♭5th	Root, ♭3rd, ♭5th, ♭7th	mi 7^{-5}, —$7^{\flat 5}$
Seventh Suspended 4th	Root, 4th, 5th, ♭7th	7 sus 4
Ninth	Root, 3rd, 5th, ♭7th, 9th	9
Minor Ninth	Root, ♭3rd, 5th, ♭7th, 9th	mi 9, $^{-}9$
Major Ninth	Root 3rd, 5th, maj. 7th, 9th	Ma 9
Ninth Augmented 5th	Root, 3rd, ♯5th, ♭7th, 9th	9^{+5}, $9^{\sharp 5}$
Ninth Flatted 5th	Root, 3rd, ♭5th, ♭7th, 9th	9^{-5}, $9^{\flat 5}$
Seventh ♭9	Root, 3rd, 5th, ♭7th, ♭9th	7^{-9}, $7^{\flat 9}$
Augmented Ninth	Root, 3rd, 5th, ♭7th, ♯9th	9+, 7^{+9}
9/6	Root, 3rd, 5th, 6th, 9th	$\frac{9}{6}$, 6 add 9
Eleventh	Root, 3rd, 5th, ♭7th, 9th, 11th	11
Augmented Eleventh	Root, 3rd, 5th, ♭7th, 9th, ♯11th	11+, 7 aug 11
Thirteenth	Root, 3rd, 5th, ♭7th, 9th, 11th, 13th	13
Thirteenth ♭9	Root, 3rd, 5th, ♭7th, ♭9th, 11th, 13th	$13^{\flat 9}$
Thirteenth ♭9 ♭5	Root, 3rd, ♭5th, ♭7th, ♭9th, 11th, 13th	$13^{\flat 9 \flat 5}$
Half Diminished	Root, ♭3rd, ♭5th, ♭7th	ø

***Note**—To arrive at scale degrees above 1 octave, (i.e. 9th, 11th, 13th) continue your scale up 2 octaves and keep numbering. The 2nd scale degree will be the 9th tone as you begin your second octave.

Order of Keys for Practicing

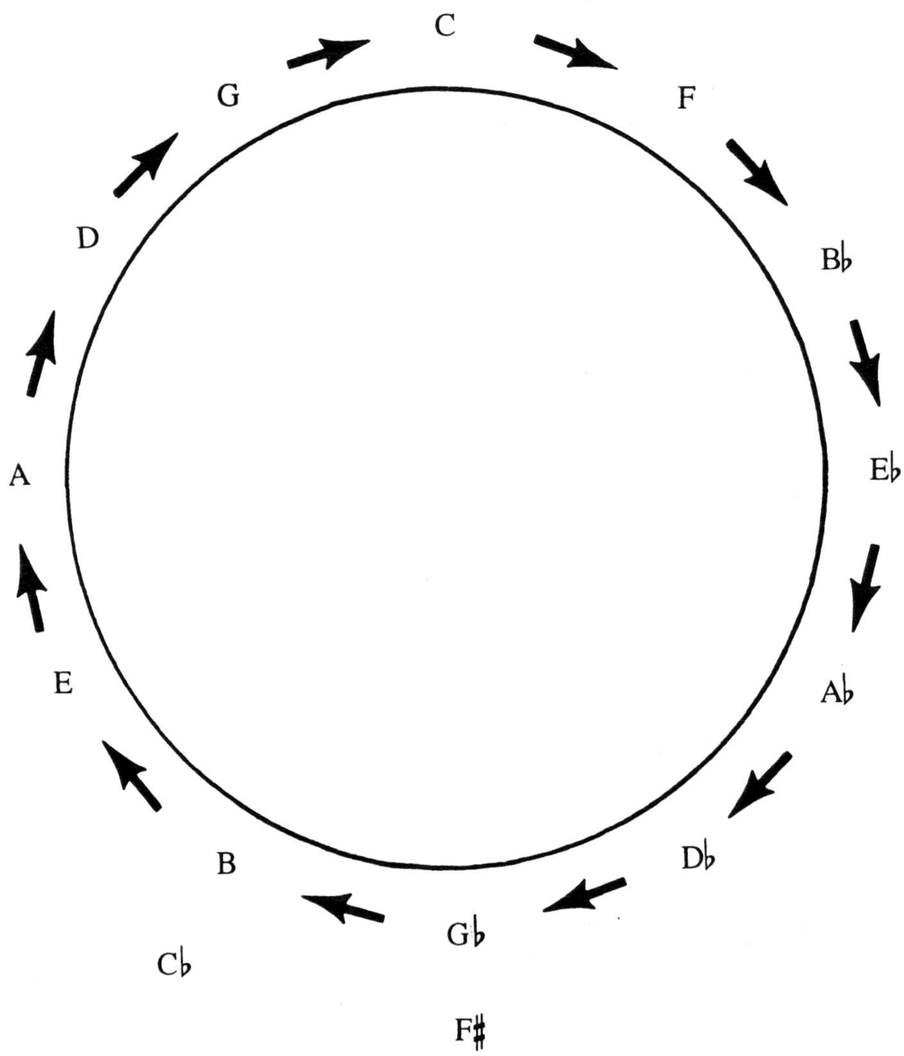

The circle is known as the "Circle of Fifths" because each tone is the interval of a perfect fifth lower than the tone preceding it.

Dominant 7th Chord

The purpose of the following studies is to train the student to hear the basic sound of the various chords. As a result, the major scale is used and altered only with the necessary chordal alterations. A complete study of scales for use against various chords when improvising will be found in the "Trumpet Improvising" section.

*The dominant seventh chord usually resolves to a fourth. (Play the arpeggio and then sing it. Singing is essential for ear training.)

Dominant 7th Scale

Study #1

Study #2

Study #3

Resolution of Dominant 7th

*As mentioned above, the dom. 7th usually resolves to a fourth (going up the scale).

Thus:

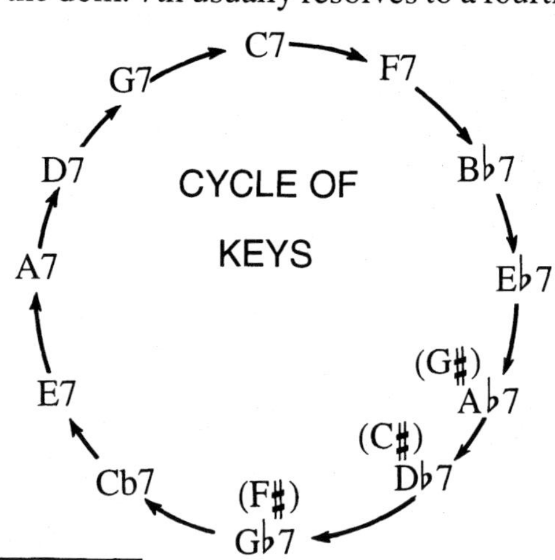

Note: Practice the above studies in all keys!

Blowin' Dom. 7th Through the Keys

For a complete study into the technical and harmonic aspects of jazz improvising, see the section on "Trumpet Improvising."

Play and sing!

Minor 7th Chord

The basic resolution of a minor 7th chord is to IV7.
Thus, Cm7→ F7.

Minor 7th Scale (Dorian Mode)

Remember to practice these studies in all keys!

Study #1

Study #2

Study #3

Study #4

Study #5

Study #6

Blowin' Minor 7th Through the Keys

Play and sing!

7♭5

The 7♭5 chord resolves usually in 2 alternate ways
1. To a 4th step thus: (C7♭5→)F
2. Or to a half step lower thus: (C7♭5→)B

7♭5 Scale

Study #1

Study #2

Study #3

Modulating Down 1/2 Step

Note: The diminished scale #2 (starting with a 1/2 step) works beautifully with a 7♭5 chord. (See page 66). This will be covered at length in the "Trumpet Improvising" section.

Blowin' 7♭5 Through the Keys

Play and sing!

Minor 7♭5

The minor 7♭5 is used frequently when improvising. It usually resolves to a dominant 7th chord and 4th above. Thus: Cmi7♭5→F7.
Play the following studies in all keys.

Minor 7♭5 Scale

Study #1

Study #2

Study #3

Common Phrase Using Mi 7♭5

Passage Ending Phrase Using Mi 7♭5

See if you can come up with your own original phrases using the mi 7♭5 chord.

Blowin' Mi 7♭5 Through the Keys

Play and sing!

Augmented 7th (7+5, 7♯5)

As with most 7th chords, the 7+5 chord resolves to a 4th above. Thus: C7+5→F

7+5 Scale

Study #1

Study #2

Study #3

Study #4–Changes Using 7+5

Note: The whole tone scale works quite well with a 7+5 chord. This will be explored later in this book, in the "Trumpet Improvising" section.

Blowin' 7+5 Through the Keys

Diminished 7th Chord (dim 7, C°)

Play and sing!

The diminished 7th chord could be called a minor 6♭5. A minor 6♭5 tends, because of the ♭5, to resolve to a fourth above. A diminished chord, however, serves as a passing chord resolving 1/2 step up or down.

Thus: Cdim ⟶ C♯7
or
Cdim ⟶ B7

A diminished chord is constructed by using minor third intervals. In order to create a scale that will work with the diminished chord, we will construct the scale on a whole step–half basis.

Diminished Scale #1

Study #1

Study #2

If we begin our diminished scale with a 1/2 step, we have a slightly different sounding scale which will work well when played against chords built on diminished type intervals. (i.e. 7♭9, 7♭9♯11;, 7♯9, or 7♯9♯11, etc.)

Diminished Scale #2

Study #1

Study #2

Study #3

Both Scales Combined

Blowin' Dim. Chord Through Keys

Study Using Diminished Scales

False Fingerings

False fingerings are used in jazz for speed and special effects. Most good jazz players utilize false fingerings quite frequently while improvising.

False Fingering Studies

Soliloquy For Miles

Easy groove

Vibrato

Vibrato is so important to trumpet style, yet very rarely is much emphasis given to it. The types and techniques of vibrato differ widely. You should listen to the types of vibrato used in various styles of music. For sheer brilliance and beauty of sound, I like to listen to Doc Severensen on big band solo work. Strangely enough, I feel that the vibrato used by the great classical soloist, Maurice Andre, is similar in pulse and brilliance. Both of these artists use a motion of the right hand as their principle means of producing vibrato. Many players use an up-and-down motion of the lower jaw to achieve the desired effect. Two artists who possess differing styles of vibrato, but who apparently use the jaw type technique are Rafael Mendez (quick pulse–brilliant sound) and the late Bobby Hacket (slower–lush sound–vibrato pulse quickens at the end of notes and phrases). The sound of this technique is sort of a breathy "woo-woo-woo" sound. For small ensemble–funky ballad type of vibrato, I like to listen to Art Farmer, Chet Baker, or Jack Sheldon.

Experiment with various techniques and sounds. Remember, your vibrato should never be mechanical. It should either sound warm and intimate or brilliant, singing, and exciting. Following are several studies. Once you can accurately control the number of pulses per measure, you will begin to be able to use vibrato in an effortless manner.

Vibrato Studies

4 Pulses Per Measure

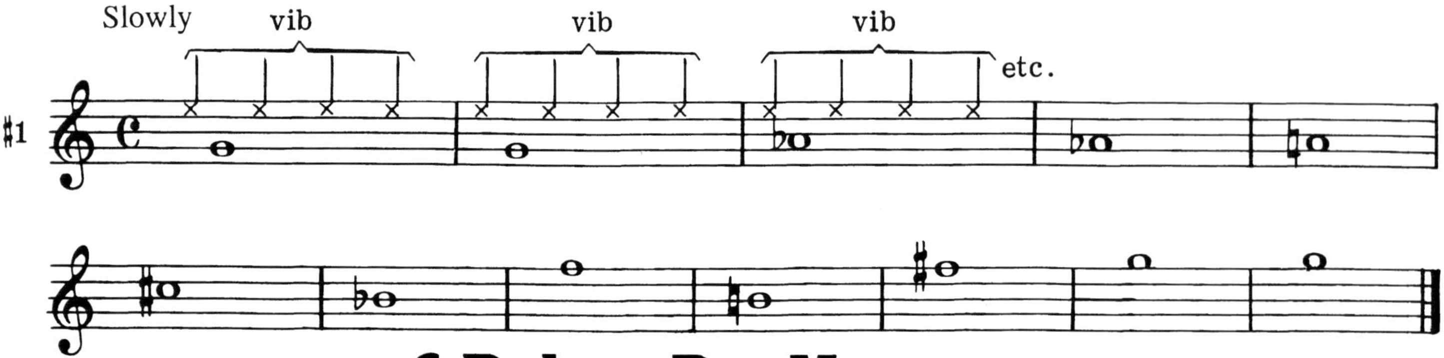

6 Pulses Per Measure

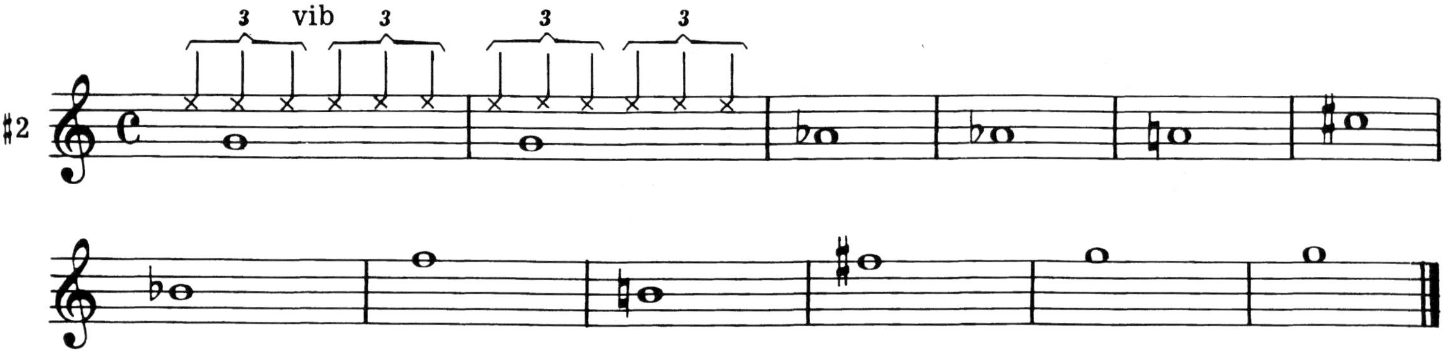

8 Pulses Per Measure

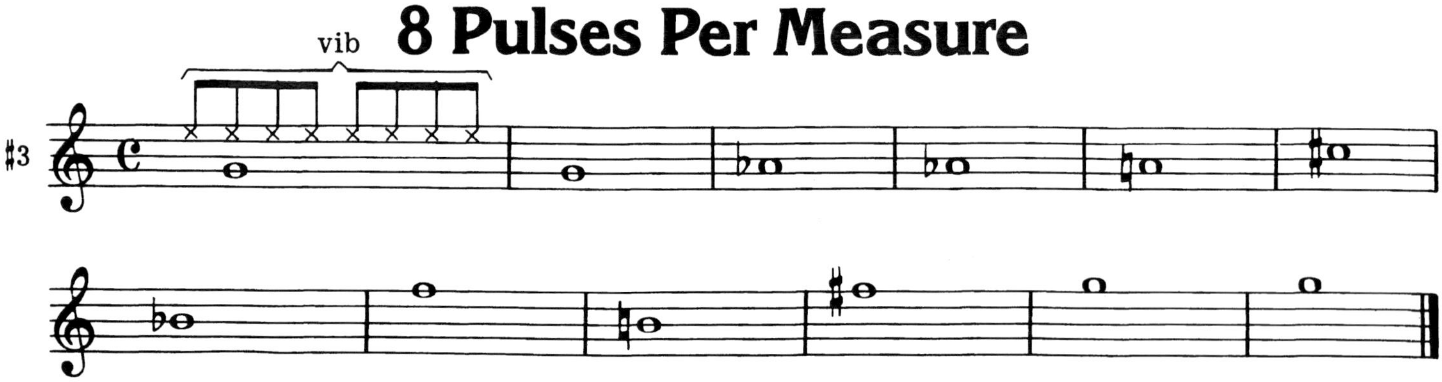

10 Pulses Per Measure

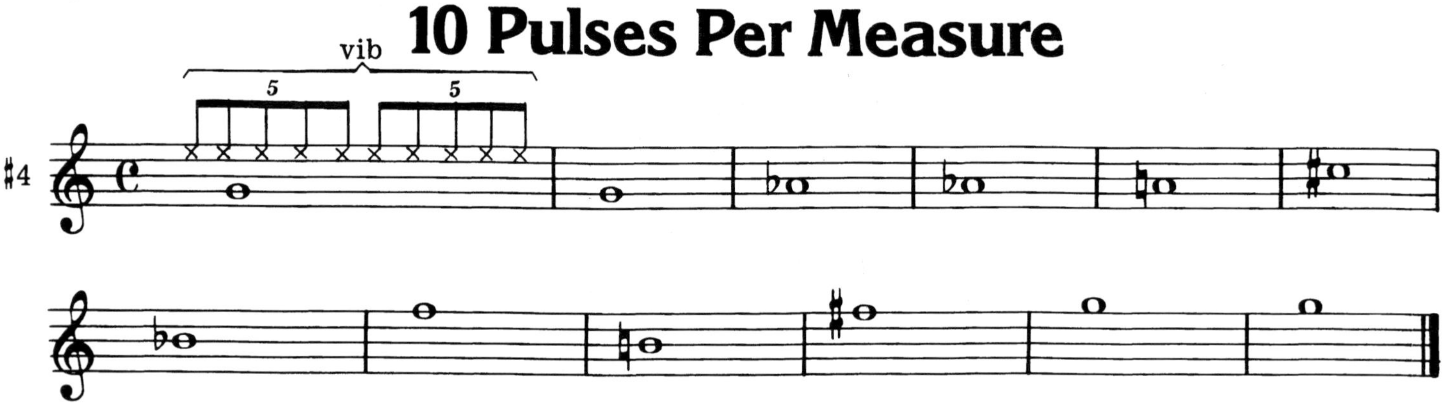

12 Pulses Per Measure

16 Pulses Per Measure

Accelerating Pulse

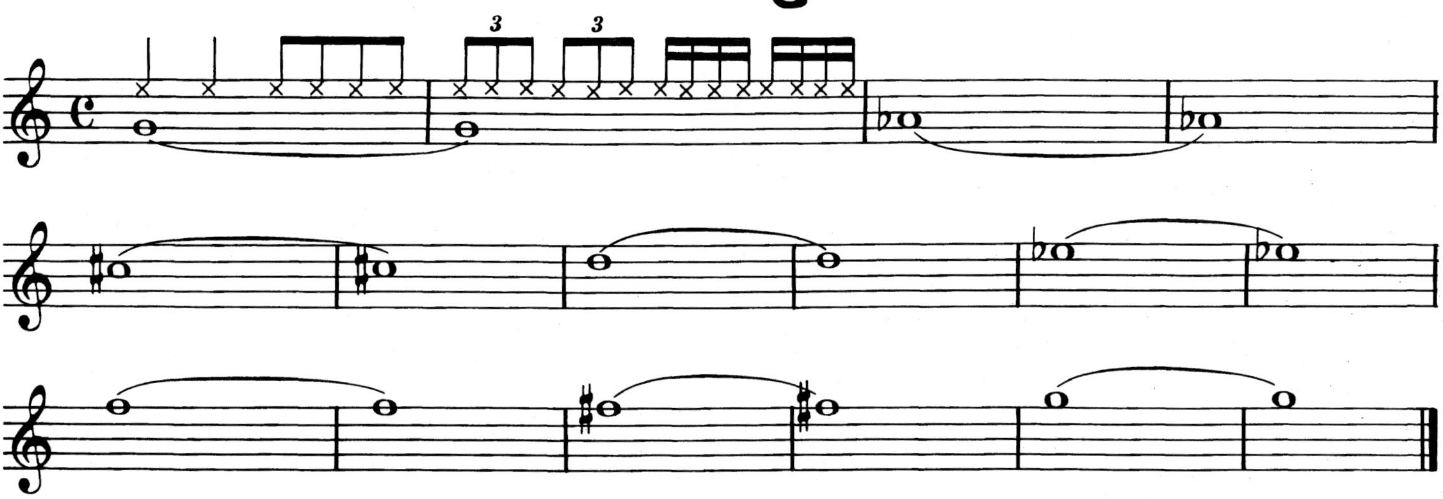

Lush Sounds

Lip Drops

Lip drops are important studies for improvisation and overall flexibility.

Study #1

Study #2

Study #3

Study #4

Wind Tolerance and Breath Control

Study #1

Range, power, and ease of playing are directly related to the control we have over air pressure. Play the following studies as effortlessly as possible. Remember to make the horn "sing."

Study #2

Study #3

Range Studies

Range and Tone Control Studies

Trumpet Improvising Workbook

This section is an in-depth study into the theory which underlies improvisational techniques. Upon completion of this book, the student should have developed both his mental understanding of chords and chord relationships.

I do recommend a careful study of the previous section, Jazz Trumpet Studies, as a prerequisite to this section. The principles laid down in the previous section will serve as a solid foundation for the advanced theory work in this volume. Ear training is emphasized throughout. I know of no better way to get into improvising than by training your ear to hear and anticipate chord progressions. I recommend the use of singing. By singing the examples presented in this text, the student will further develop the ear. I also recommend taking up the guitar or another keyboard instrument as a means of developing the ear to hear chord changes. A trumpet player is greatly enhanced if he has a chordal instrument as a second instrument. The guitar seems to be a natural. I know many trumpet players who adapted to the guitar quite easily.

In this text, do each part thoroughly. Do not skip any sections and do not rush through the material. Take your time. Master each section thoroughly. Remember, it takes time to train your ear. Upon completion of this book, the student should be quite ready to move into good improvisation ideas. Listen to as many good players as possible. This is how you get ideas. Apply the ideas you hear on records to the principles involved in this text.

Scale Building

Scales are the foundation on which chords are built. If you can picture a building, think of scales as the foundation on which the building rests; think of chords as the framework which gives the building its structure and strength; and think of improvising as the use of various construction materials, design, landscaping, etc. which gives the building its style. We will begin with the major scale.

Major Scale

A major scale is a series of eight notes arranged in a pattern of whole steps and half steps.

C Major Scale

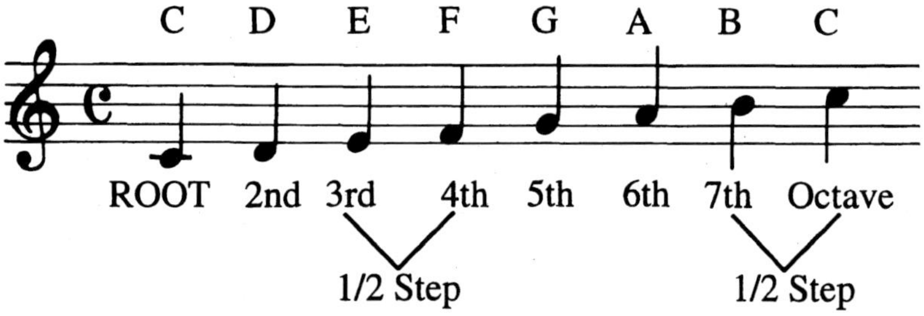

C to D	=	Whole Step
D to E	=	Whole Step
E to F	=	1/2 Step
F to G	=	Whole Step
G to A	=	Whole Step
A to B	=	Whole Step
B to C	=	1/2 Step

To construct a major scale we first start with the name of the scale (frequently called the Root or Tonic). With the C scale this would be the note "C". The rest of the scale would fall in line as follows:

Scale Tones		Distance From Preceeding Note
Root	(C)	
2nd	(D)	Whole Step
3rd	(E)	Whole Step
4th	(F)	1/2 Step
5th	(G)	Whole Step
6th	(A)	Whole Step
7th	(B)	Whole Step
Octave	(C)	1/2 Step

With the above formula you can construct any major scale!

G Major Scale

To construct the G major scale, start with the note G, construct it as follows:

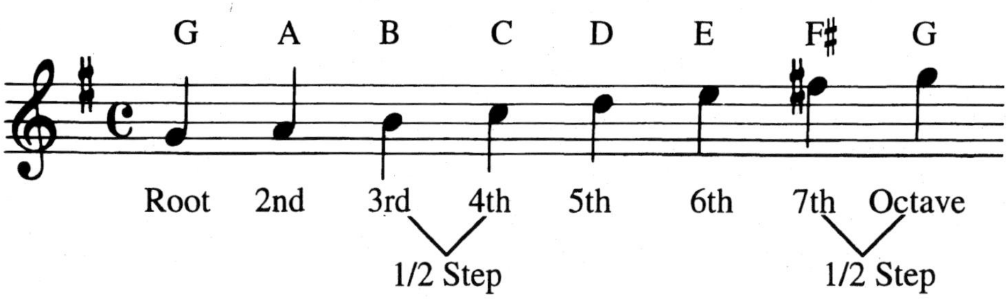

Notice that in order to make our formula work with the G scale we must sharp (♯) the F. There must be a whole step between the 6th and 7th tones of the scale. In order to establish a whole step between E and F we must sharp the F.

Constructing Major Scales

Construct the major scale for each key and label the Root, 3rd, and 5th tones of each scale. Finally, write the sharps or flats found in each key.

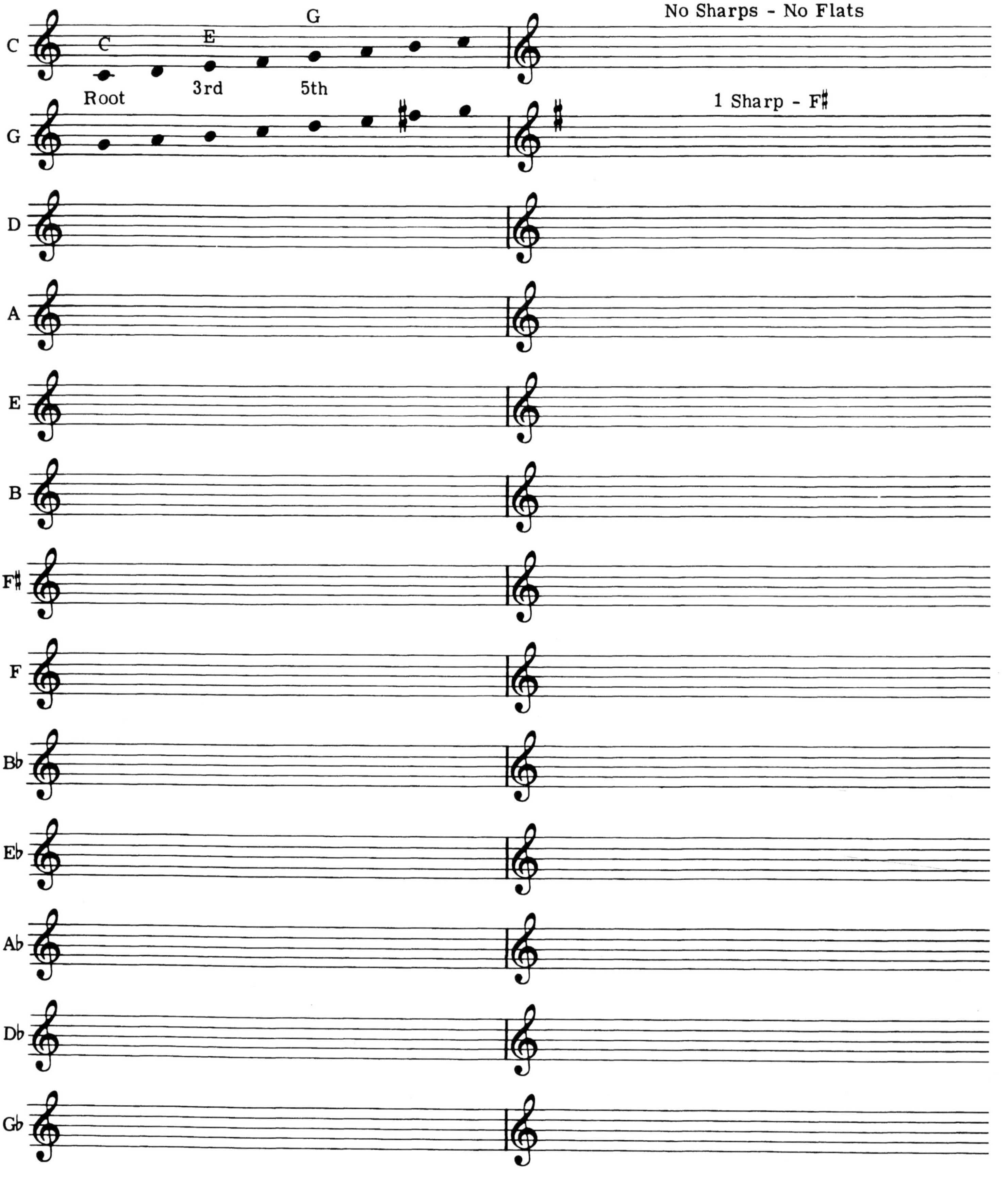

Major Chords

A major chord is comprised of the Root, 3rd, and 5th tones of a scale. The notes in the C major chord would be C-E-G. The notes in the G chord are G-B-D.

Write the notes of the major chords and label as follows:

Example:

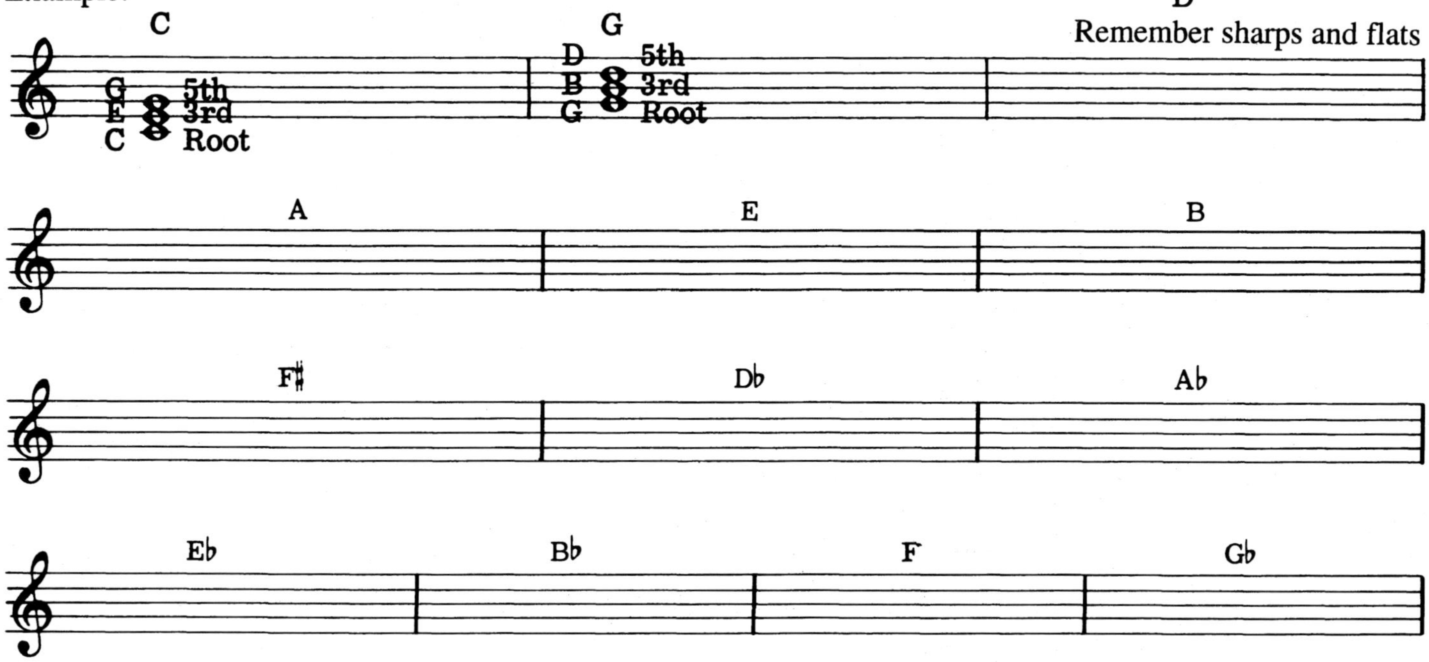

Sing and Play

Sing and Play the following major chords. (Sing Root-3rd-5th. Play Root on your instrument to check your pitch.)

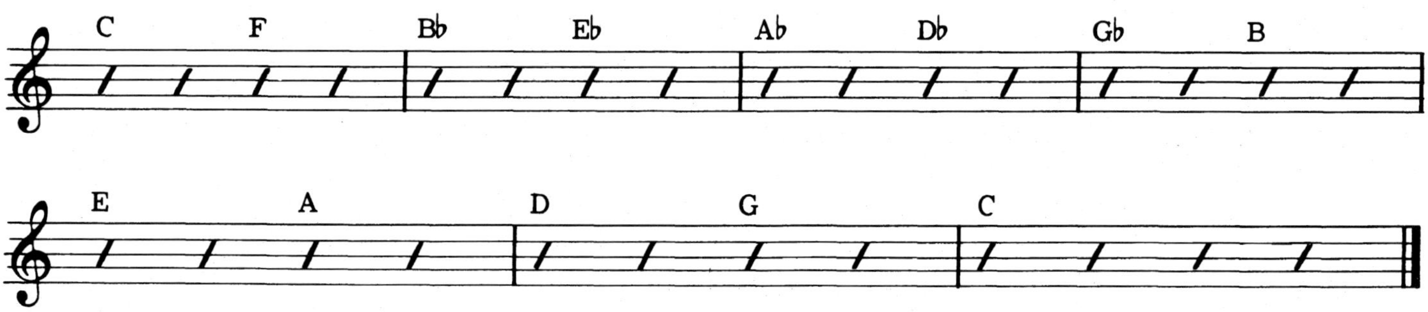

Inversions

Inversions are the different ways in which a chord may be written or played: That is to say, a "C" chord may be constructed:

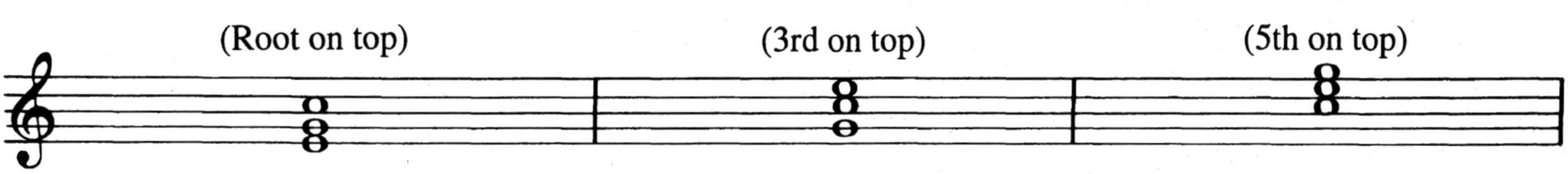

Melodic Development on Major Chords

In order to really learn to hear chords, it is valuable to experiment with short melodic phrases built on the corresponding scales. Below are several examples. Play and sing them through the various keys. Next, **invent your own**. Write them down and play and sing them through the keys like the following example.

Example #1

Example #2

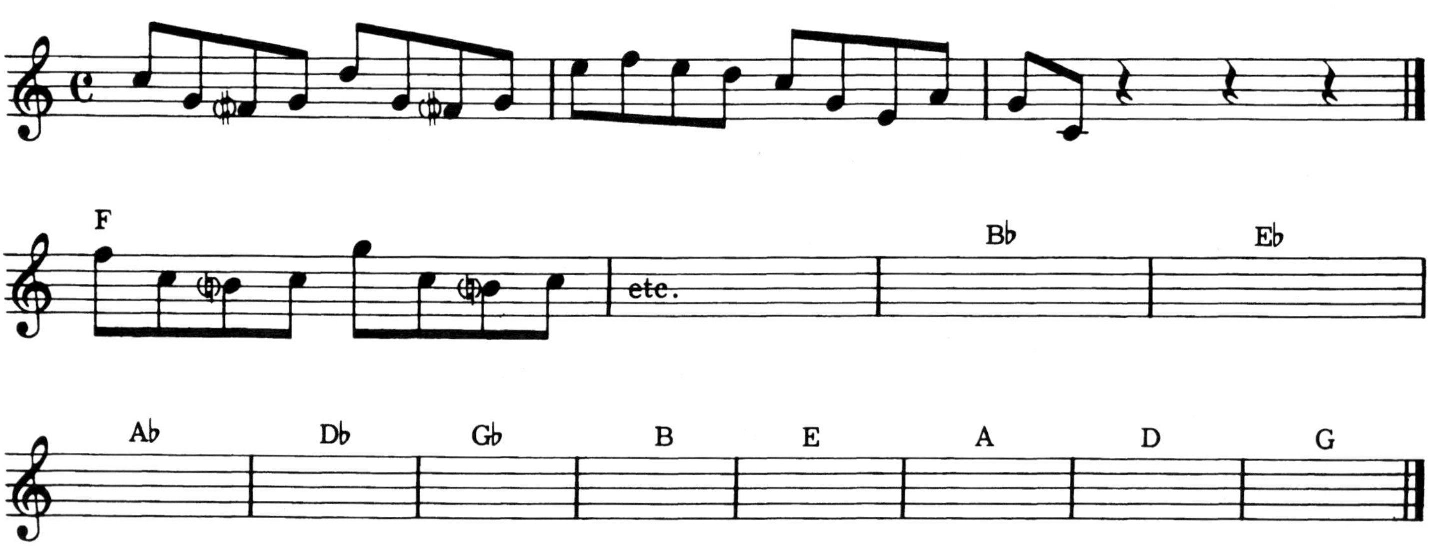

Write Your Own

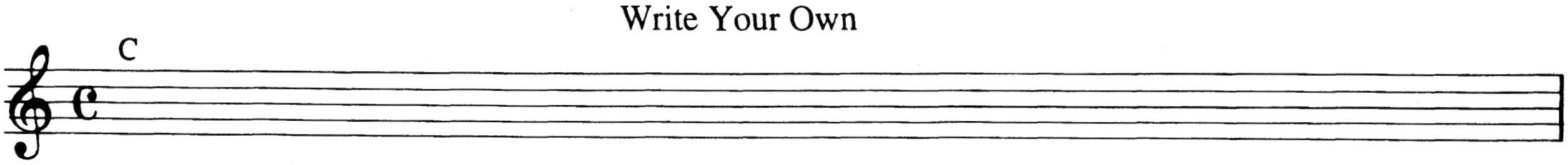

Write, Sing, and Play

Write and Sing the Following Chords

Scale Relationships

In order to understand, analyze and play chord progressions, you need to learn what chords are built on the various scale degrees of a given key.

Scale Degrees

(Key of C)

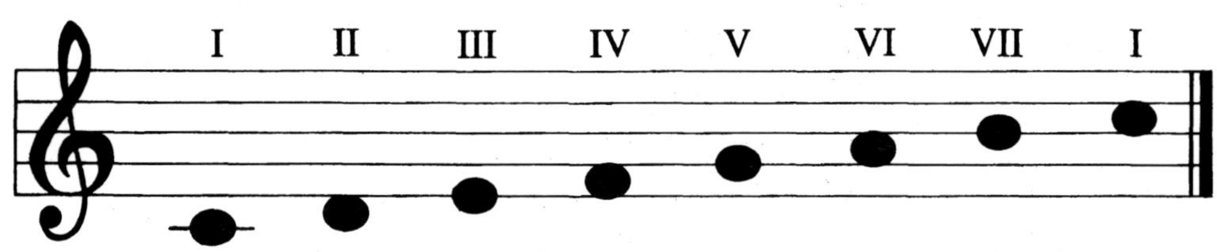

Thus, the IIm chord in the key of C would be Dm. The V^7 chord in the key of G would be D^7. The $IIIm^7$ chord in the key of D would be $F\sharp m^7$.

Write the answers to the following questions and spell out the appropriate chords.

1. The IMa^{7} chord in the key of D♭ is _____.
2. VIm^{7} in key of A is _____.
3. V^{9} in key of G is ______.
4. IIIm^{7} in key of C is _____.
5. Vm^{7} in key of D is _____.
6. VIm^{7} in key of B is _____.
7. IVm^{9} key of B is _____.
8. IM$^{7-5}$ in key of G is _____.
9. IM^{7} in key of F♯ is _____.
10. IVMa^{7} in key of F is _____.
11. IImi^{7} in key of A is _____.
12. VII$^{\circ}$ in key of C is _____.
13. ♭Vm^{7} in key of G is _____.
14. ♭IIIm^{7} in key of E is _____.
15. IVMa^{9} in key of A is _____.
16. V^{7} add 6 in key of E is _____
17. II^{11} in key of G is _____.
18. VIm^{7} in key of F is _____.
19. ♭IVm^{7} in key of C is _____.
20. V$^{7=5}$ in key of E is _____.
21. IIIm in key of A is _____.
22. ♭IIIm in key of G is _____.
23. II^{7} in key of D is _____.
24. II^{6} in key of B is _____.
25. IVm^{6} in key of D is _____.
26. IIma^{7} in key of B is _____.
27. Vmi^{7} in key of A is _____.
28. VImi^{7} in key of A is _____.
29. IIImi^{7} in key of E is _____.

Beginning Progressions

While many approaches exist for teaching improvisation, I feel it is most beneficial to:

1. Study chord construction.
2. Study chord resolution.
3. Study chord substitution.
4. Study alternate scales to be used against chords.

Cycle of Fifths

The basic movement of chords in our western music is according to the cycle of fifths. Study the chart below. It could be called the Cycle of Fourths because each chord resolves to a chord built on a 4th scale degree. Thus, C leads to F; or (to put it another way) C is the V chord of F.

Cycle of Fifths

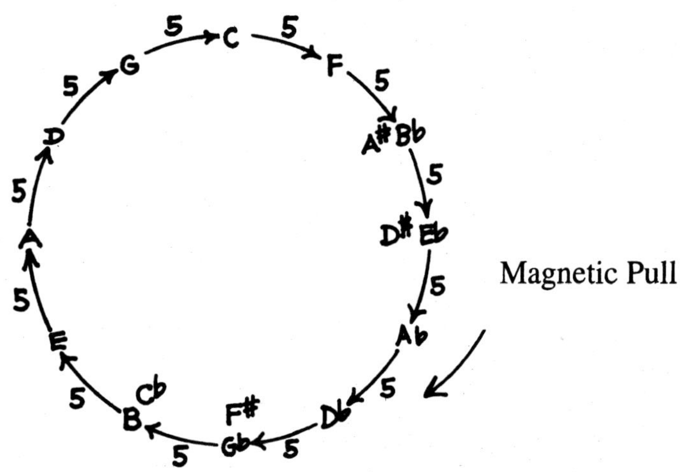

EXERCISE

C leads to _____(F)	D leads to_____
B♭ leads to _____	G leads to _____
A♭ leads to _____	G♭ leads to _____
E leads to _____	F leads to _____
A leads to _____	B leads to _____
D♭ leads to _____	E♭ leads to _____

Dominant 7th Chord

Remember:
The dominant 7th chord resolves to a fourth step above.
Thus: $C^7 \rightarrow F$ $G^7 \rightarrow C$ etc.

V7 to 17

The above pattern started on the 5th of the V7 chord. Write your own pattern starting on the 3rd, then starting on the root, then starting on the 7th.

Your Pattern Starting on the 3rd

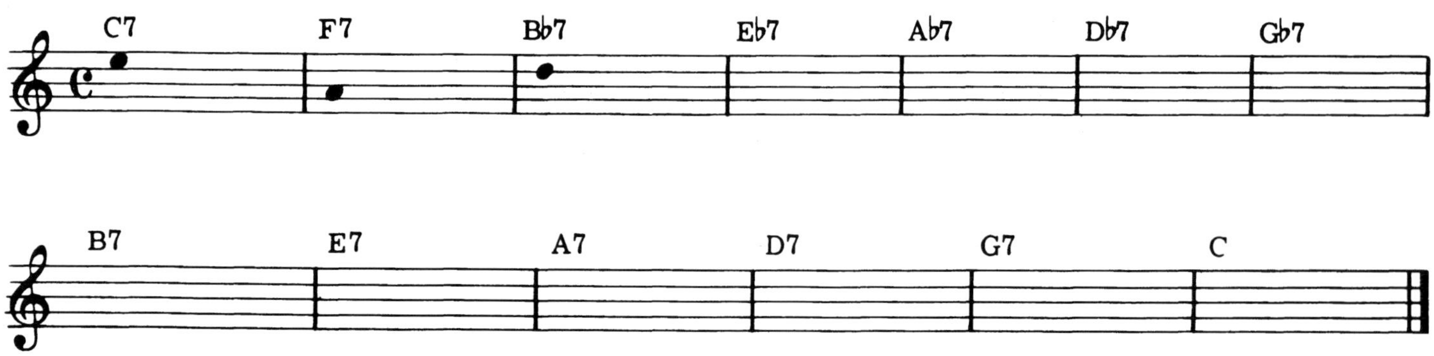

Now write and play patterns starting on Root, then the 7th.

Blues Scale

The blues scale works well against major, minor, or 7th chords. The formula for building blues scales is:

Root	-	♭3rd, whole step, 1/2 step, 1/2 step, ♭3rd interval, whole step.
Root	-	♭3rd, 4th, ♭5th, ♮5th, ♭7th, Root
C	-	E♭, F, G♭, G, B♭, C

Play the following keys:

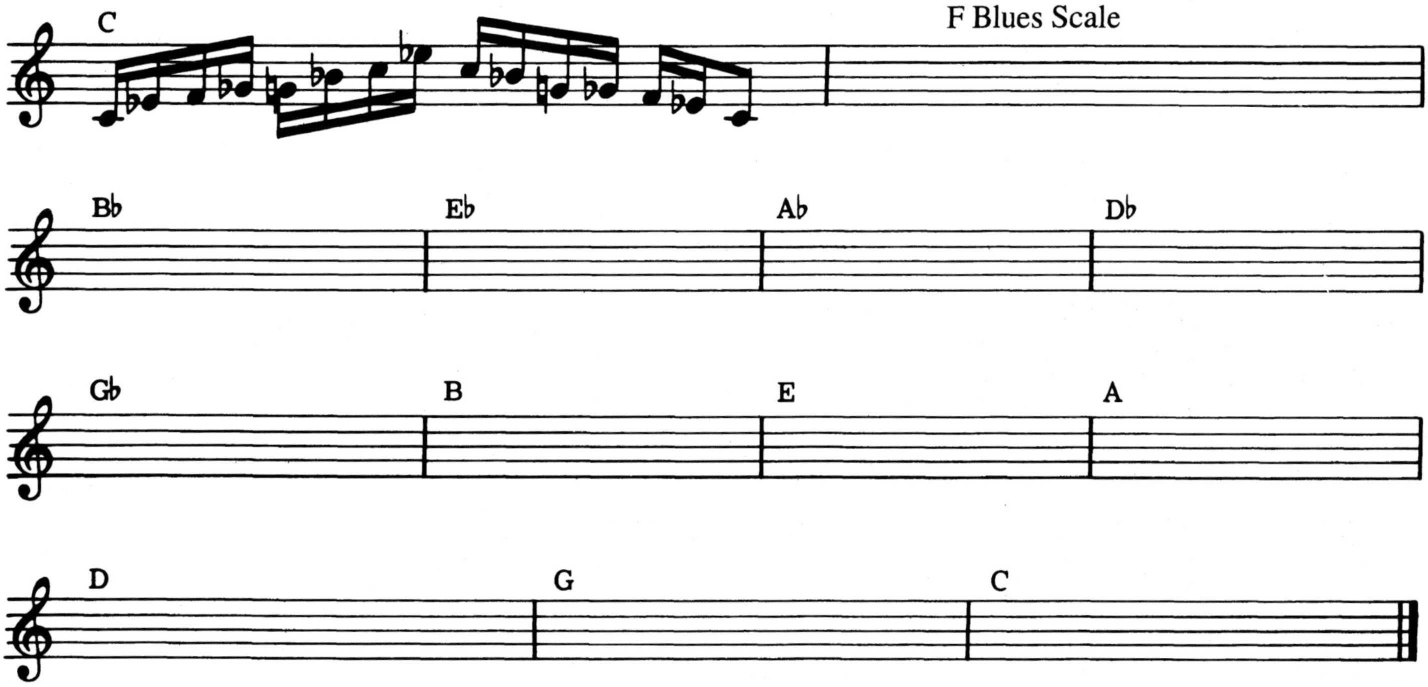

Blues Modulation

C7 Blues Scale

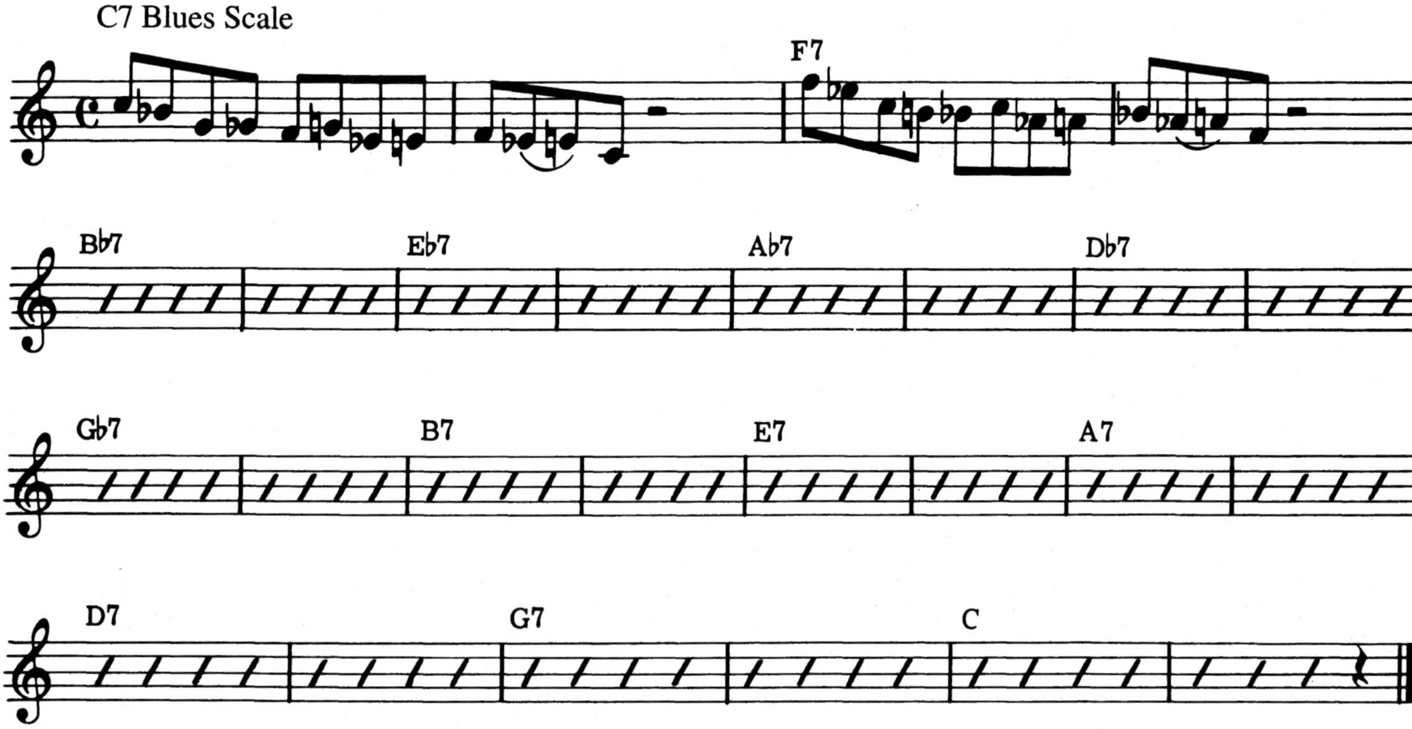

Melodic Ideas-Blues Scale

You should be keeping a notebook of your own ideas on phrases to be used against certain chords. Also, you should now begin to try and play solos you hear and like off of recordings. This is great ear training and will really help both your ear and style. **Play the following ideas in all keys.** Then, as usual, **write some of your own.** The more you write and play, the greater will be your progress. Play the following studies by ear through the cycle of keys.

1. 

Play in all studies in F, B♭, E♭, A♭, D♭, G♭, B, E, A, D, G.

2. 

3. 

4. 

5. 

Rock tempo

6. 

7. 

V7 to I Using Blues Scale

The blues scale can be played against the dominant or minor seventh type chords. The use of the blues scale in such situations is governed by style and taste. Play the following examples and write your own ideas.

Continue by ear in E♭^{7} → A♭, A♭^{7} → D♭, D♭^{7} → G♭, G♭(F#)^7 → B, B^7 → E, E^7 → A, A^7 → D, D^7 → G.
Write the studies in all keys if you have trouble at this stage playing them by ear.

Continue the above study by ear in F^7 → B♭, B♭^{7} → E♭, E♭^{7} → A♭, A♭^{7} → D♭, D♭^{7} → G♭, G♭(F#)^7 → B, B^7 → E, E^7 → A, A7 → D, D7 → G.

Write Your Own

Write your own studies on V7 to I using the blues scale. Play each study by ear in all keys!

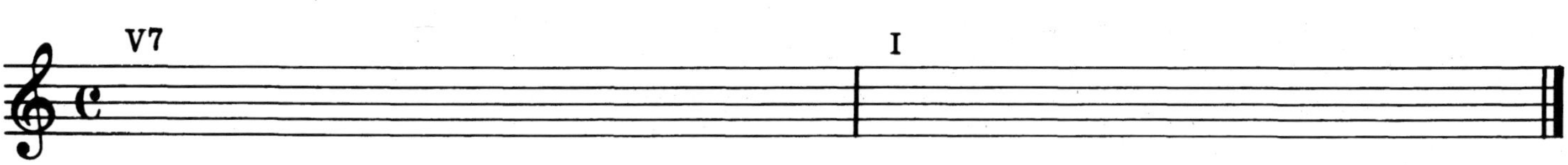

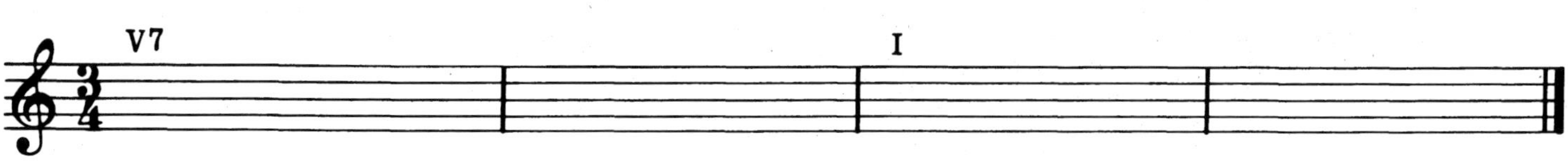

Expanding Our Basic V7-I Progression

II7 → V7 → I

Play all of the following examples by ear through the cycle of keys!

1.

Play above in keys of F, B♭, E♭, A♭, D♭, G♭, B, E, A, D, G, C.

2.

3.

Rock feeling

4.

Playing Arpeggios

A good way to learn to hear a new progression is to simply play the chords in arpeggio form. Try the following.

Play all of the above exercises and **make up your own** in all keys.

VI7-II7-V7-I

Play the following in F, B♭, E♭, A♭, D♭, G♭, B, E, A, D, &G.

1. 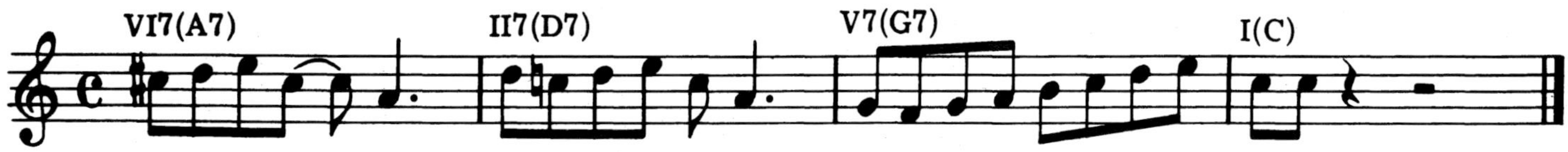

2. 

3. 

4. 

5. 

Write Your Own

On all progressions covered in this section, the more you write, the better will be your playing!

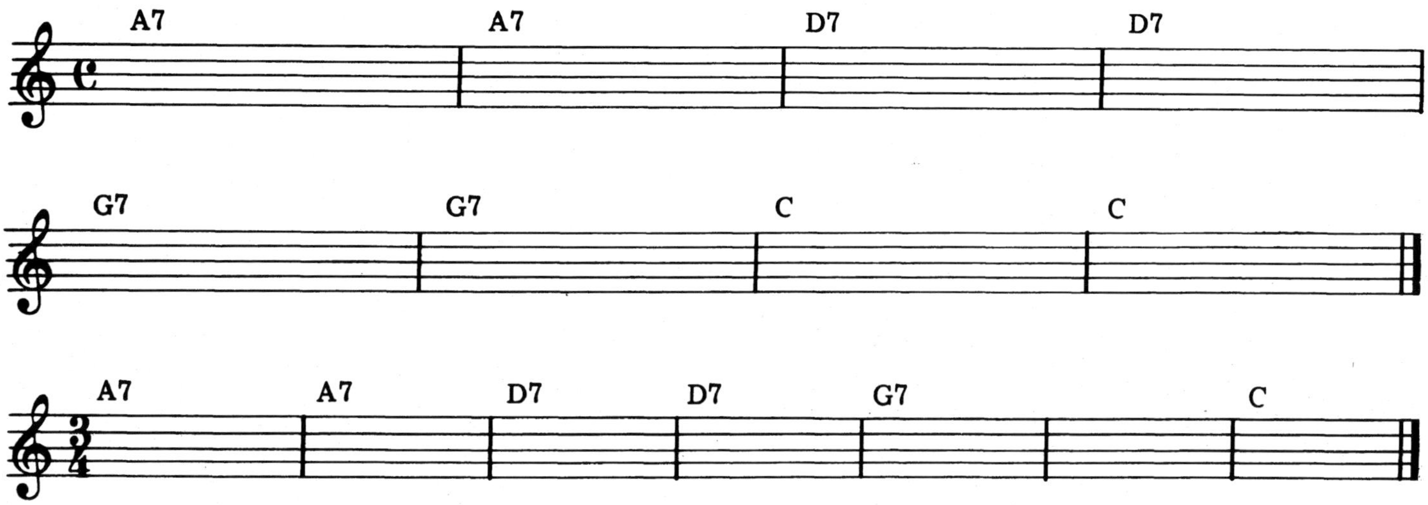

Review Study

Write the correct chord or progressions.

1. IV in key of C
2. V^7 in key of A♭
3. I in key of F♯
4. VI^7—II^7 in B♭
5. II^7—V^7 in D♭
6. IV—V^7 in E♭
7. V^7 in F
8. II^7—V^7 in G
9. IIIm in A
10. VII^7 in E
11. III^7—VI^7 in D♭
12. VIm—IIm—V^7 in B
13. $IIIm^7$—VI^7—II^7—V^7 in G♭
14. VI^7—♭VI^7—V^7 in C
15. ♭III^7—II^7—♭II^7 in E♭
16. $IIImi^7$—VI—II^7—V^7 in A
17. VIm—IIm—V^7 in F
18. IVm^7—$IIIm^7$—♭$IIIm^7$—IIm—V^7 in A♭
19. VII^7—III^7—VI^7——II^7—V^7—I in D
20. III^7—II^7—♭III^7—I in G

I-III7-VI7-II7-V7-I

Play the above studies in: F, B♭, E♭, A♭, D♭, G♭, C♭, E, A, D, G.

Write Your Own

(The more-the better! Play them in all keys by ear!)

Write Another

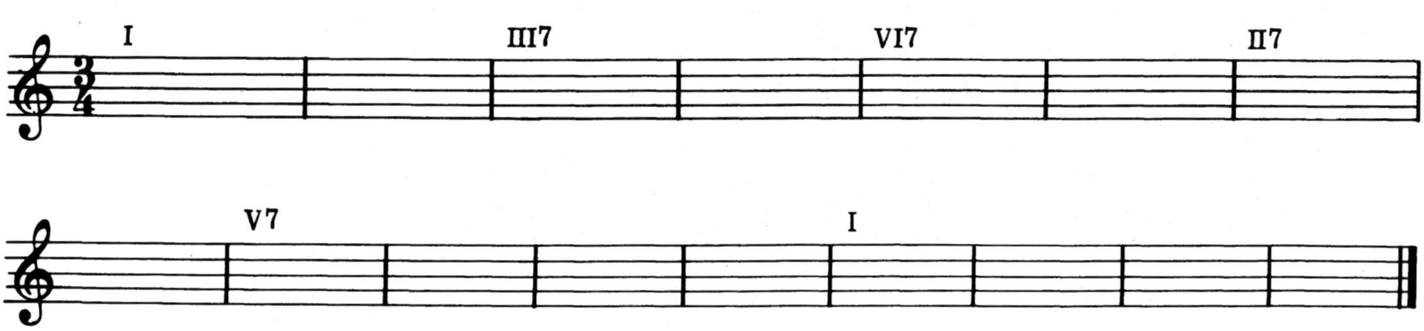

Minor Chords

Many different minor scales exist. All may be used with varying degrees of effectiveness against chords in the minor family. We will deal here with the ascending melodic minor scale and the dorian mode.

Play and Sing

Play and Sing
C Melodic minor scale (Ascending)

Assignment

1. Play the following studies.
2. Play them again by ear but this time transpose them up 1/2 step. Keep doing this until you have played the studies by ear in all keys. (Example— The following study uses C melodic minor. Next, fake the same study in D♭ minor next D minor, etc.)
3. Write your own studies using the melodic minor scale and fake them by ear in all keys by moving either up or down chromatically.

Melodic Minor Study

Play by ear in Fm, B♭m, E♭m, A♭m, D♭m, G♭m, Bm, Em, Am, Dm, Gm.

Simple Progression

Play in all keys.

Melodic Development On Melodic Minor

You need to experiment with the melodic minor scale. Below are several ideas. Play them by ear in all keys. Keep a note book of your own ideas and learn them in all keys. Alter the rhythms to give your ideas variety.

Play also in Am, Em, Bm, G♭m, D♭m, A♭m, E♭m, B♭m, Fm, Cm, Gm.

Dorian Mode

Play and Sing

The dorian mode is scale which follow the minor 7th chord very closely. To construct the notes of the dorian mode, count down 2 half steps. Whatever sharps or flats appear in the major scale built on this tone will be used to construct our dorian mode.

Constructing a Dorian Mode

By counting down 2 half steps we get B♭. Therefore, we will now play the C major scale with B♭ and E♭ (The accidentals in the key of B♭) to have our dorian mode starting on C.

Dorian Mode

Formula for dorian in steps

Root	- whole -	1/2 -	whole -	whole -	whole -	1/2 -	whole
C	D	E♭	F	G	A	B♭	C

Write the Following Dorian Modes

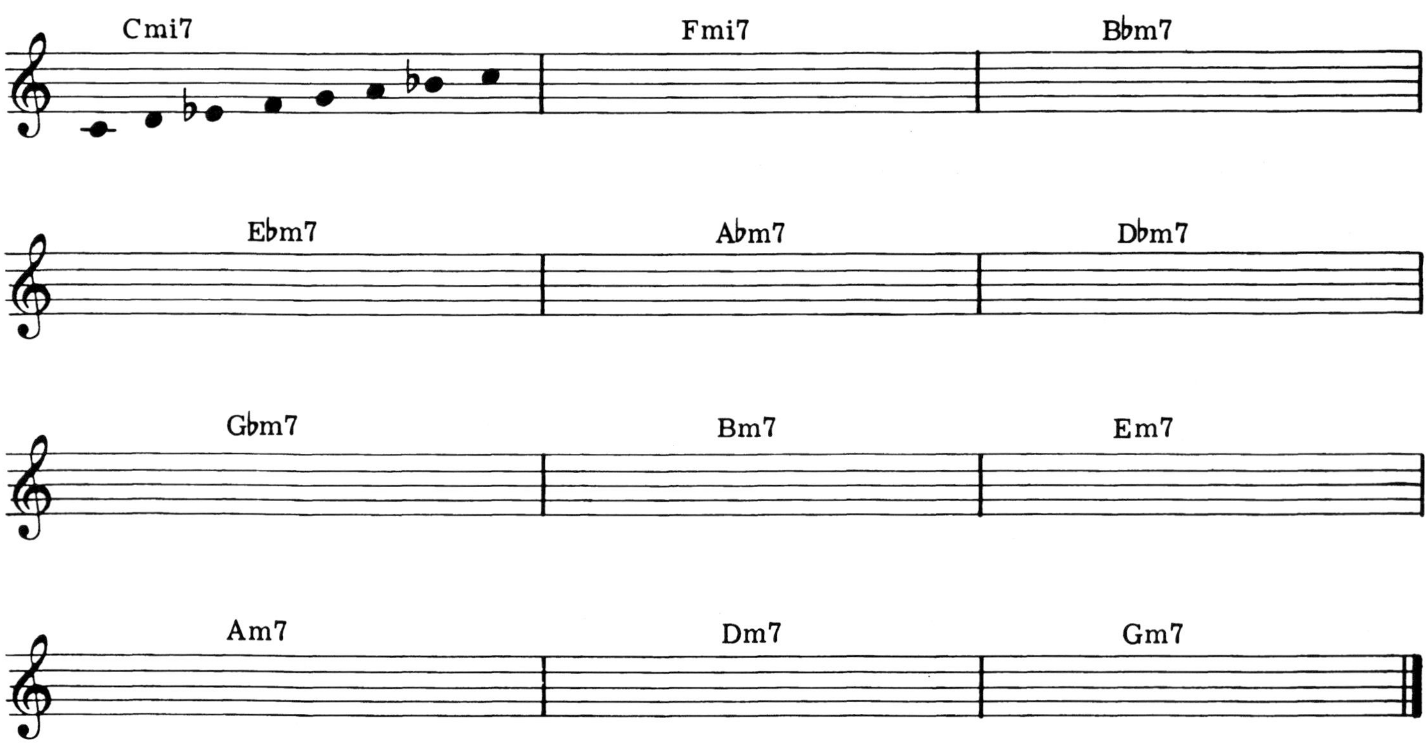

Melodic Development on Dorian Mode

Here are some ideas using the dorian mode. Play them in all keys and write your own ideas. The more you write, the better will be your progress.

Play in all keys of Dm, Gm, Cm, Fm, B♭m, E♭m, A♭m, D♭m, G♭m, Bm, Em, Am.

1. 

2. 

3. 

4. 

5. 

6. 

7. 

8. 

Pure or Natural Minor

(Also know as Aeolian Mode)

The formula for building pure minor scales is as follows. Find the 6th tone of a major scale and continue through eight letters of that major scale. If we take the C scale for example, we will find that A is the 6th tone of the C scale. If we then start with A and continue for eight notes, we will have the A pure minor scale.

Example: C Scale "A" Minor Scale

A is 6th tone in C scale

"A" minor is said to be "Relative" to C. (A is the 6th tone in the C scale and the A minor scale is built on the scale starting with A.) A table of major keys and their relative minor keys follows:

The Major and Relative Minor Keys

D is the 6th tone of the F scale; G is the 6th tone of the B♭ scale, etc.

F	Dm	F♯	D♯m
B♭	Gm	B	G♯m
E♭	Cm	E	C♯m
A♭	Fm	A	F♯m
D♭	B♭m	D	Bm
G♭	E♭m	G	Em

Finding Relative Minor

To find the relative minor key to any given major key, count down three half steps. When you begin playing chord progressions, you will see how frequently the relative minor appears. Thus, it is important to recognize it.

Relative Minor Key Quiz

1. The Am scale is relative (or built on) the _____scale. (Answer C)
2. The Dm scale is relative is relative to the ______scale.
3. The Ebm scale is relative to the ______scale.
4. The Gm scale is relative to the _____ scale.
5. The C#m scale is relative to the _____scale.
6. The G#m scale is relative to the _____scale.
7. The Cm scale is relative to the _____scale.
8. The Fm scale is relative to the _____scale.
9. The Em scale is relative to the _____scale.
10. The F#m scale is relative to the ______scale.
11. The Bbm scale is relative to the _____scale.
12. The Ebm scale is relative to the _____scale.
13. The Bm scale is relative to the _____scale.

Major to Pure Minor

(Relative)

Play and Sing

Write and Play

Continue

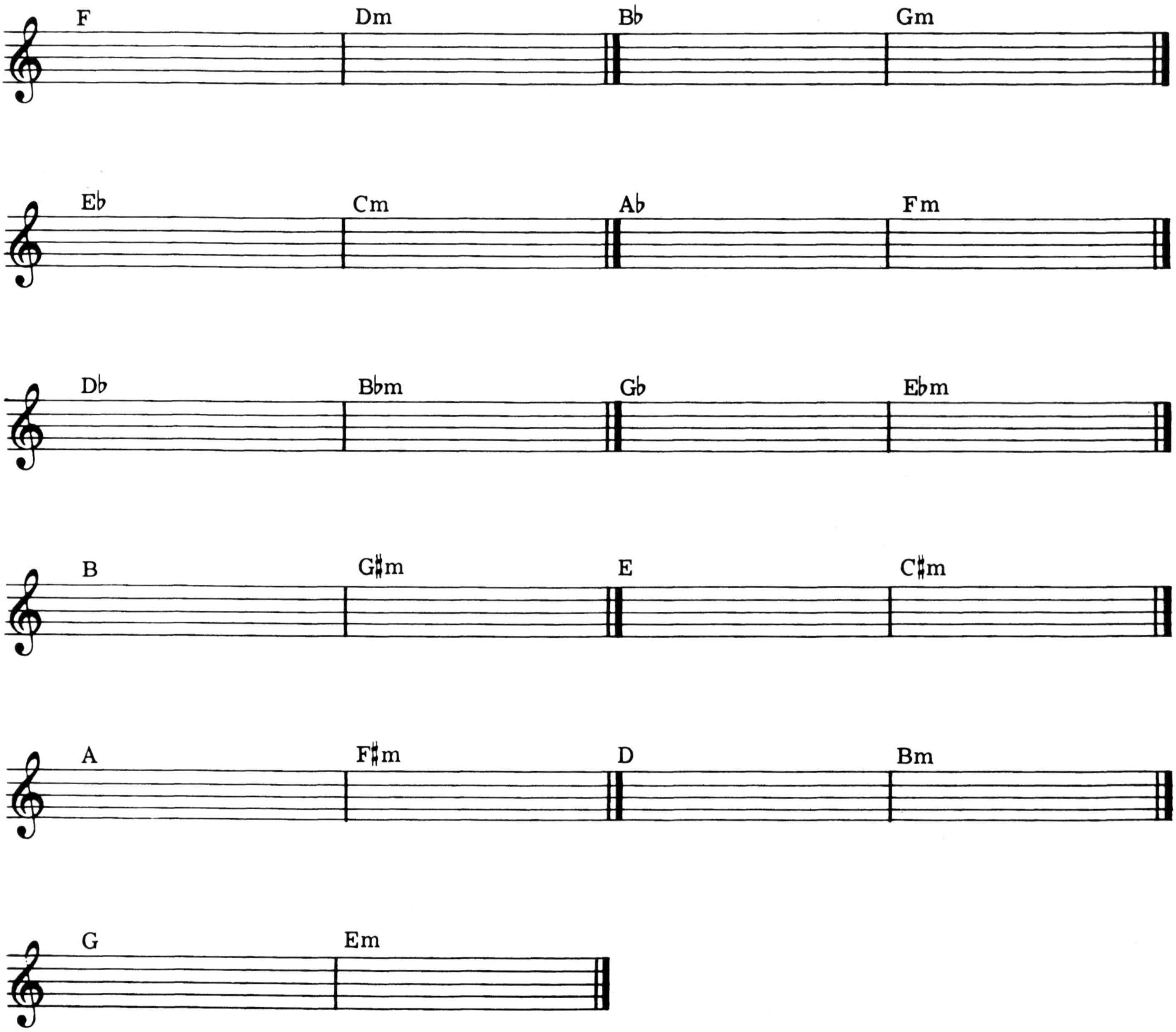

Play the Scale that Corresponds to the Following Chords

Practice the following study by:

First—Playing the scale which corresponds to the chord
Second—Play each chord for extended periods, improvising on the appropriate scale tones.

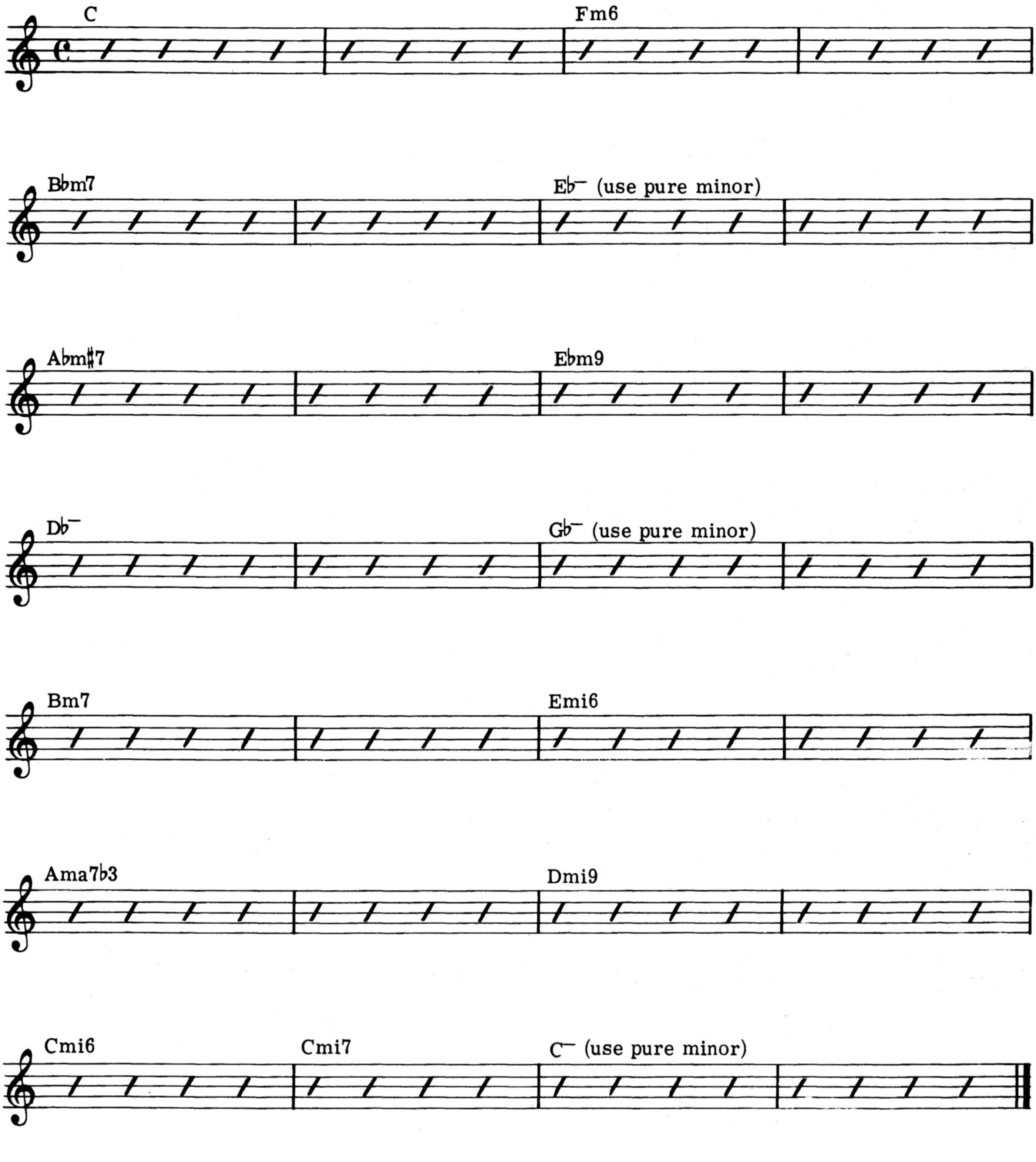

Dorian to Blues

The blues scale works well against the dominant or minor 7th chords. In the following example, we will alternate between the dorian and blues scale.

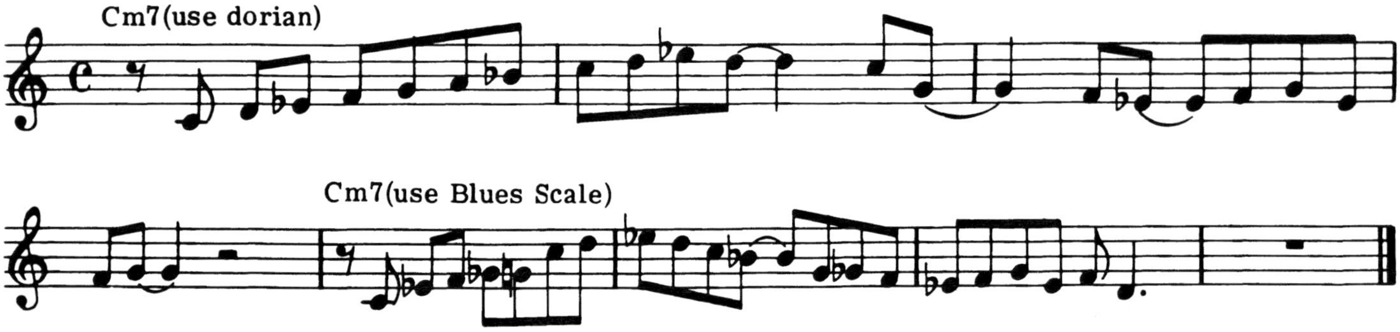

Play Your Own Ideas

Dominant 7th Scale

(Mixolydian Mode)

There are 2 ways that we can think of a scale which fits a Dominant 7th Chord.

1. We can flat the 7th tone of a given major scale.

   or

2. We can think in terms of the Mixolydian mode.
   To construct a mixolydian mode, count up a 4th and play in that key.
   For example: In the key of C, F would be a 4th above C. Therefore, the C mixolydian scale would be a scale from C to C using the accidentals found in the key of F.

Another Way of Thinking

I find the easiest way of thinking of a scale to use against the dom. 7 chord is to count up a 5th and to play a dorian mode built on that scale tone. Thus:

Thinking this way has the advantage of indirectly forcing you to emphasize the 5th, 7th, 9th, and to some extent, the 11th of the C7 chord.

Play scales and scale patterns that correspond to the following chords. Write your ideas.

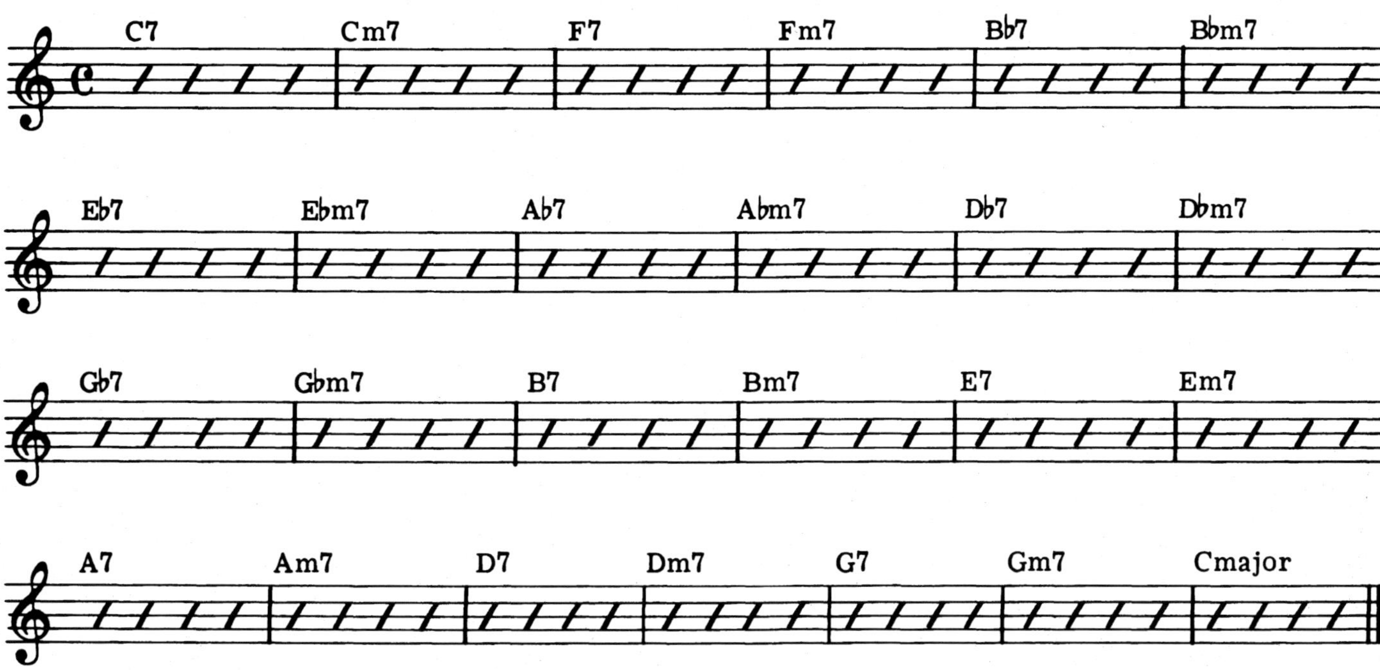

Melodic Studies on Dominant 7th

Once again, 1. Play the following studies by ear in all keys.
2. Write your own melodic ideas and play them in all keys.
Remember: A dominant 7th chord resolves up a fourth step.
Thus: C7 → F; F7 → B♭; A7 → D; etc.

Play C7 → F; F7 → B♭; B♭7 → E♭; E♭7 → A♭; A♭7 → D♭; D♭7 → G♭; G♭7 → C♭ or (B); B7 → E; E7 → A; A7 → D; D7 → G;G7 → C.

1. 

2. 

Can modulate to relative minor of F (Dm)

3. 

4. 

5. 

Play Changes

6. 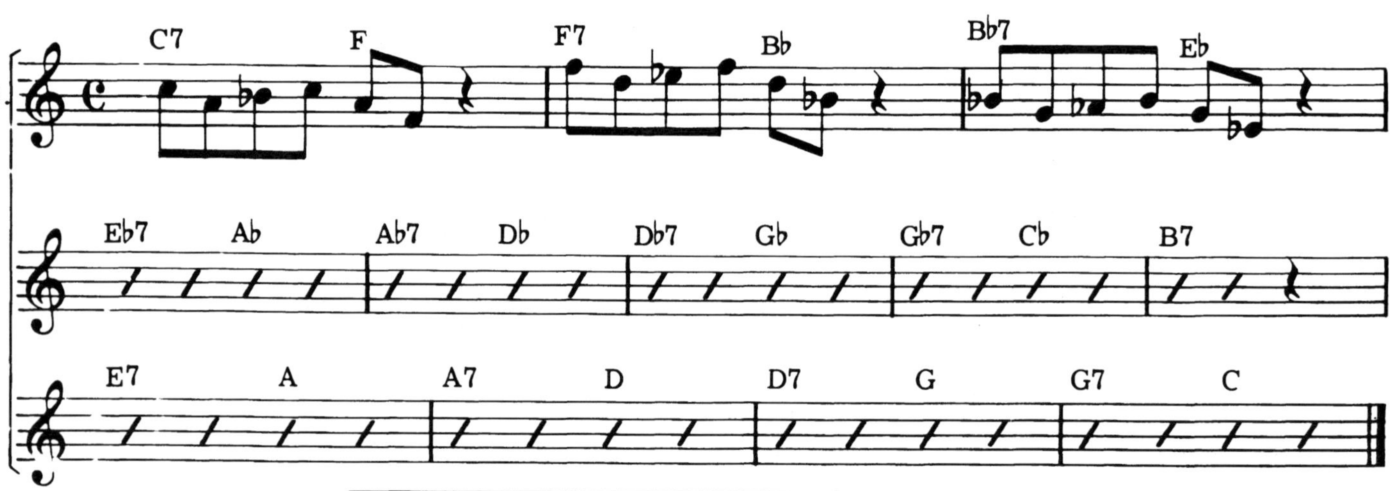

Now play study number 6 going from Dom. 7 to minor

Example  Continue

Vmi7 to I7

The Vmi7 to I7 is a basic progression to jazz and blues. Below are some phrases showing this. Play them by ear in **all keys.** Following this study, write and play your own.

Play above by ear going down chromatically, G♭7 → B7; Fm7 → B♭7;Em7 → A7; E♭m7 → A♭7;Dm7 → G7; D♭m7 → G♭7; Cm7 → F7; Bm7 → E7; B♭m7 → E♭7; Am7 → D7;A♭m7 → D♭m7.

Play Your Own Vm7 to I7

Write out choruses and have a pianist, guitarist, etc. . . play the chords while you improvise.

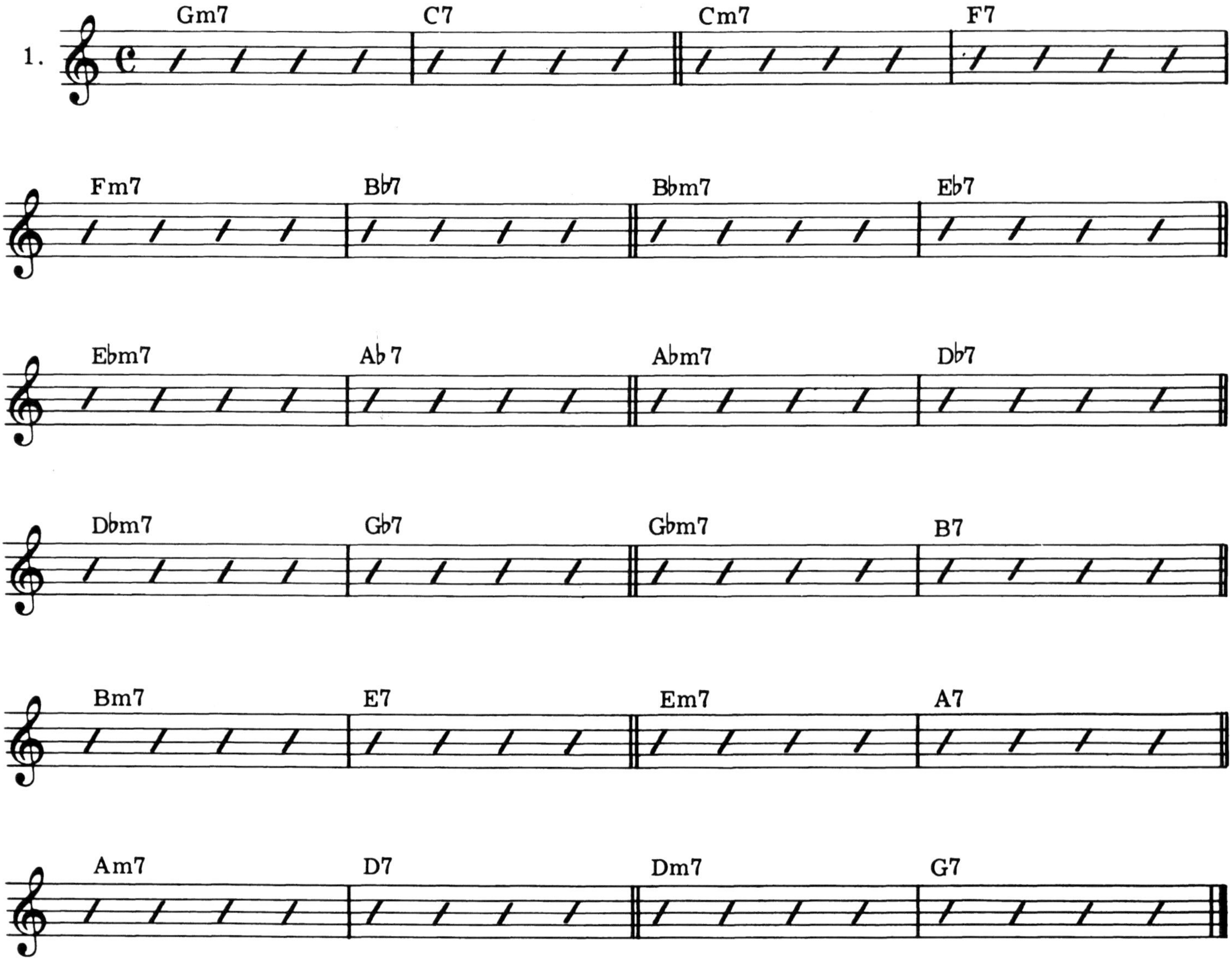

Another Study

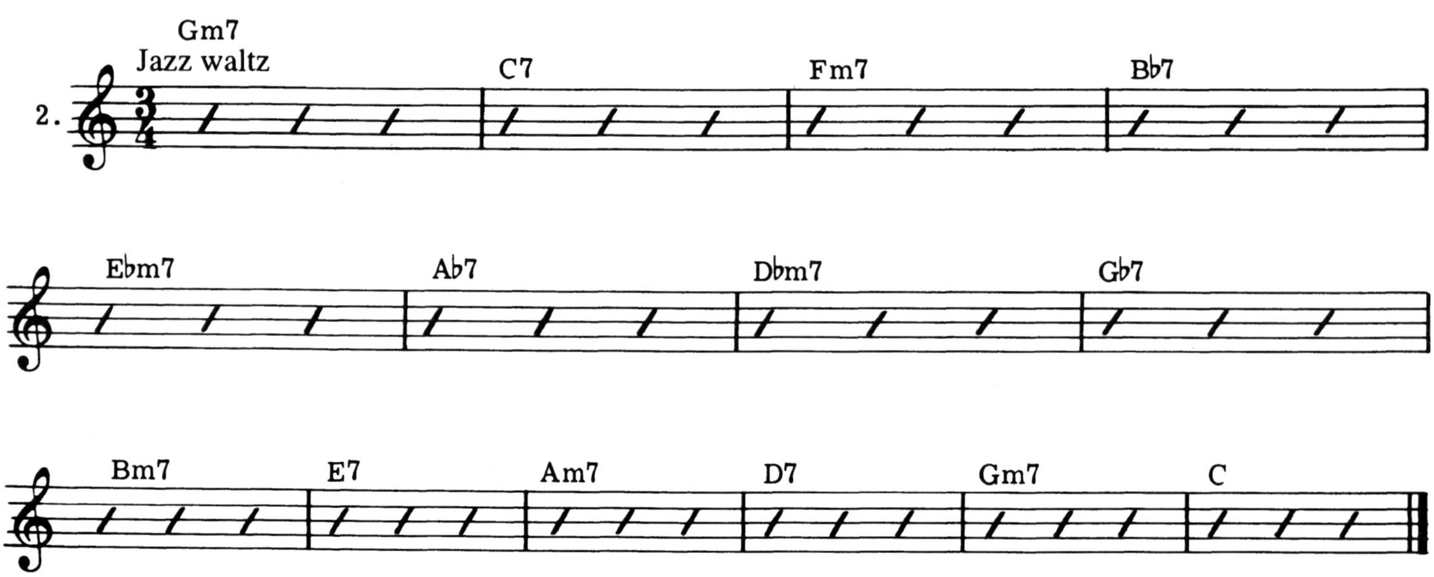

The Half Diminished Scale

The half diminished scale is useful to know because you can frequently use it against a minor 7th chord. Actually a half diminished chord (ø) is a minor 7♭5. There is an important distinction in how it resolves.

When playing a chord progression and a minor 7♭5 chord appears, the resolution will be up a 4th. (Cm7♭5 → F or Fm7♭5 → B♭)

If a half diminished chord appears, the resolution is usually to a diminished of the same root tone or to another chord of the same root. (Dma7 → Dø → D° or Cø → Cma7)

Half Diminished Scale

(Locrian Mode)

The formula for a ø scale is Root-1/2 step-W-W-1/2-W-W-W

Write and Play the Following Scales

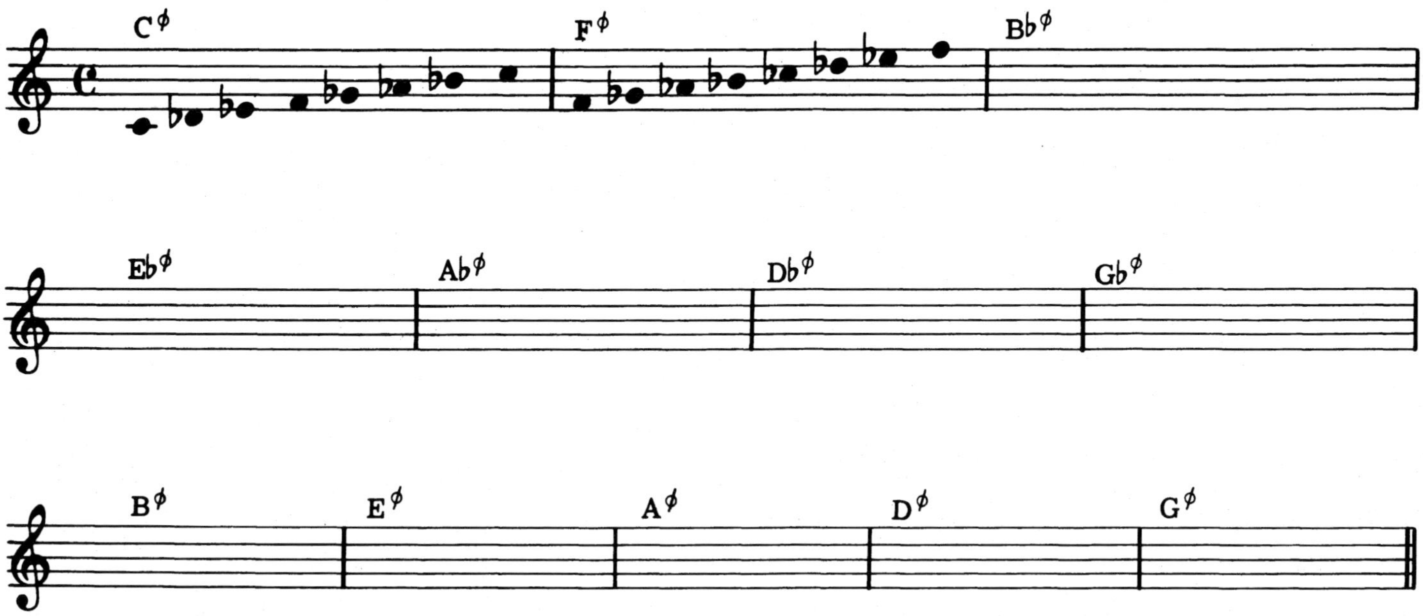

Minor 7 to ∅ Study

Play above by ear in B♭m, E♭m, A♭m, D♭m, G♭m, B♭m, Em, Am, Dm, Gm..

Continue in Fm, B♭m, E♭m, A♭m, D♭m, G♭m, Bm, Em, Am, Dm, Gm.

Continue in Fm, B♭m, E♭m, A♭m, D♭m, G♭m, Bm, Em, Am, Dm, Gm.

Continue the above in Fm, B♭m, E♭m, A♭m, D♭m, G♭m, Bm, Em, Am, Dm, Gm.

Continue the above in Fm, B♭m, E♭m, A♭m, D♭m, G♭m, Bm, Em, Am, Dm, Gm.

Write Your Own Study and Play in All Keys

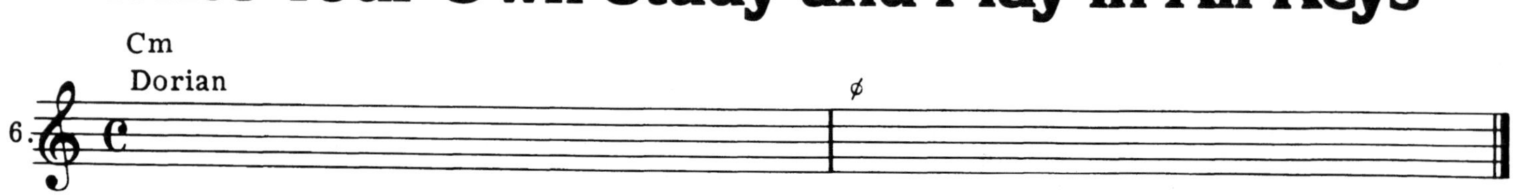

Play Your Own Vm7 to I7

(Use half diminished scale for the minor 7 chords)

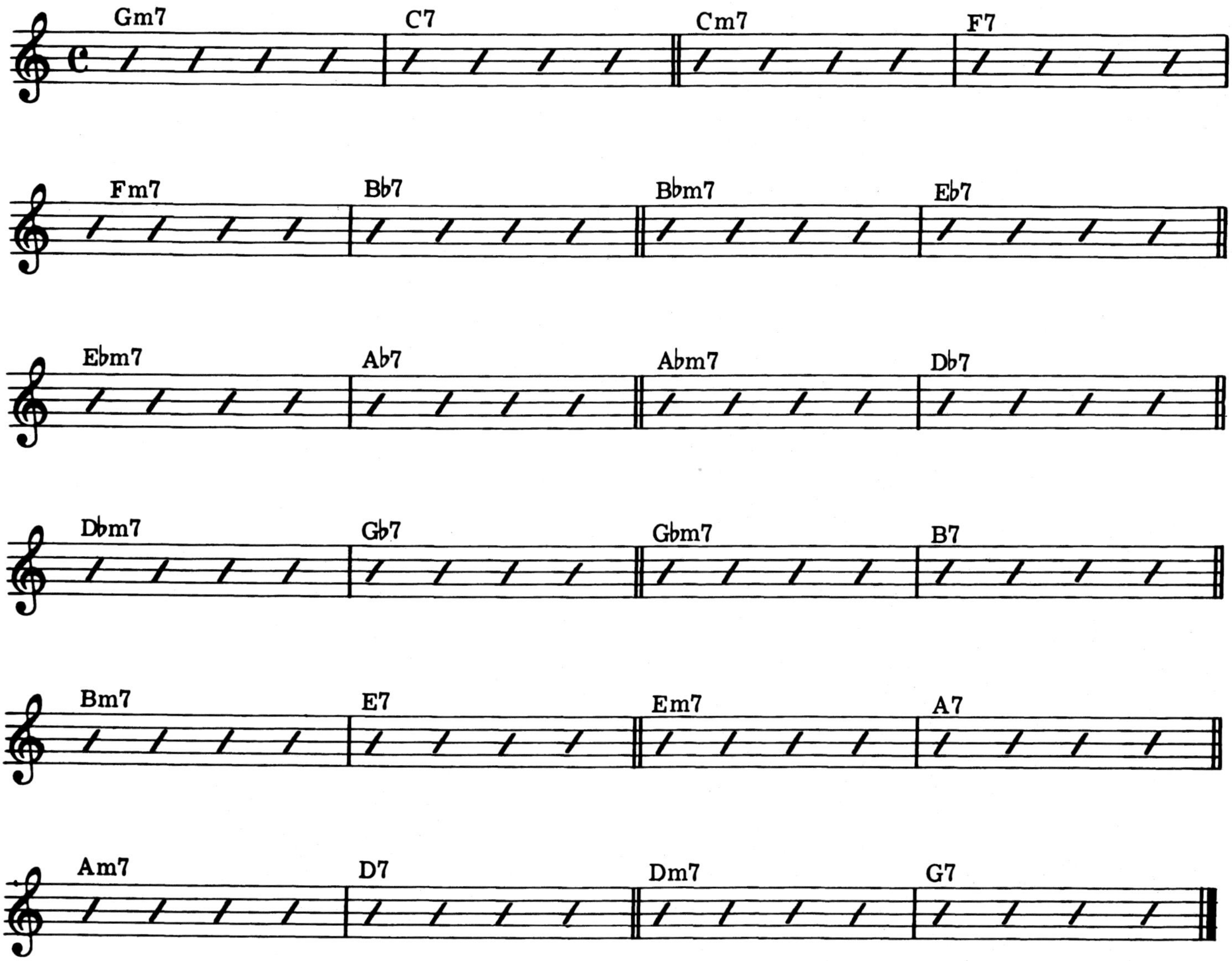

Another Study

Jazz waltz

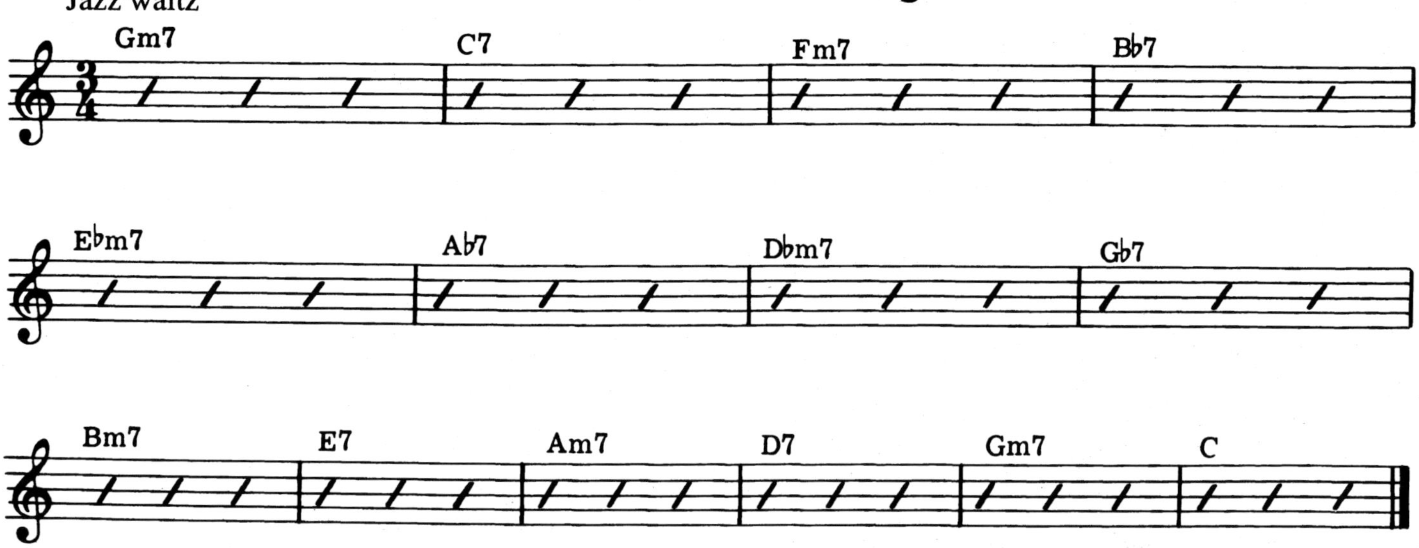

Diminished 7th Chord

(dim7)

The diminished 7th chord could be called a minor 6♭5. A minor 6♭5 tends, because of the ♭5, to resolve to a fourth above. A diminished chord, however, serves as a passing chord resolving 1/2 step up or down.
Thus: Cdim. → C♯7
Cdim. → B7

Dim. 7 Scale

A diminished chord is constructed by using minor third intervals. In order to create a scale that will work with the diminished chord, we will construct the scale on a whole step-half step basis.
The formula for diminished scale #1 is:

Root	Whole step	1/2 step	Whole step	1/2 step	Whole step	1/2 step	Whole step	1/2 step
C	D	E♭	F	F♯	G♯	A	B	C

Diminished Scale #1

Study #1

Study #2

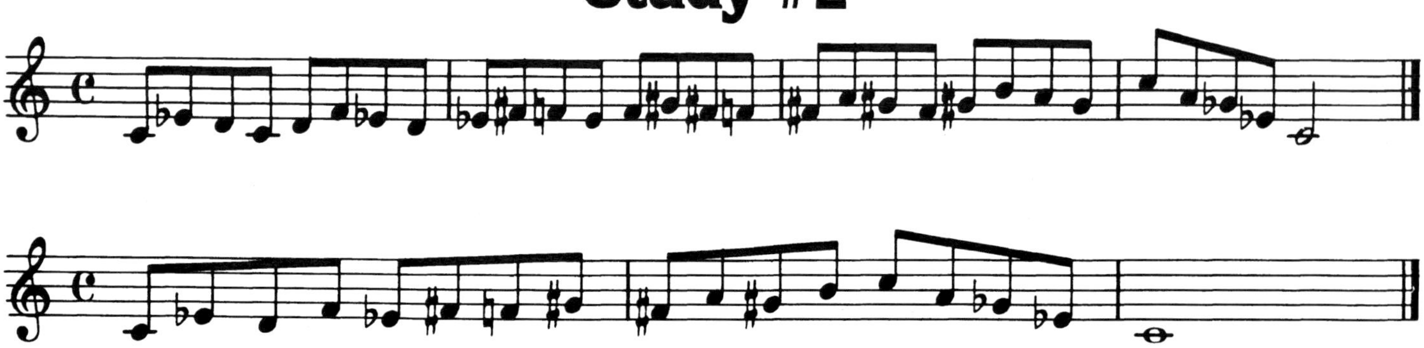

I-#I°-IIm7-V7

Write Your Own and Play in All Keys

Write Another

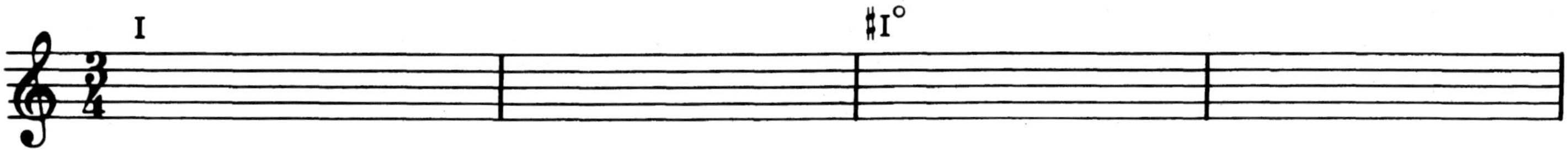

I-♭III°-IIm7-V7

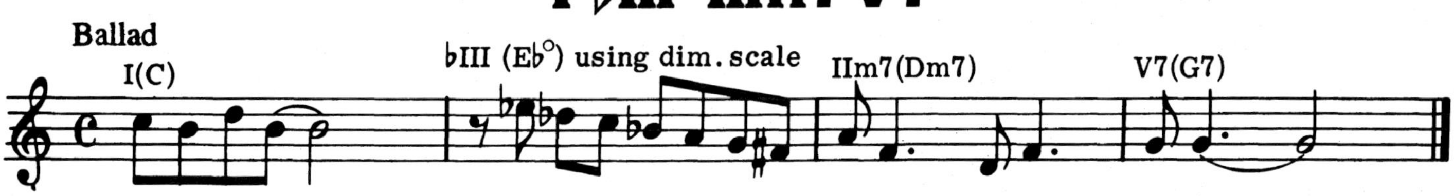

Write Your Own and Play in All Keys

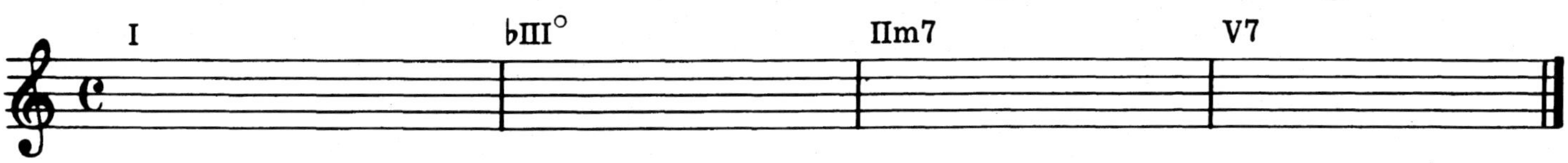

Write Another

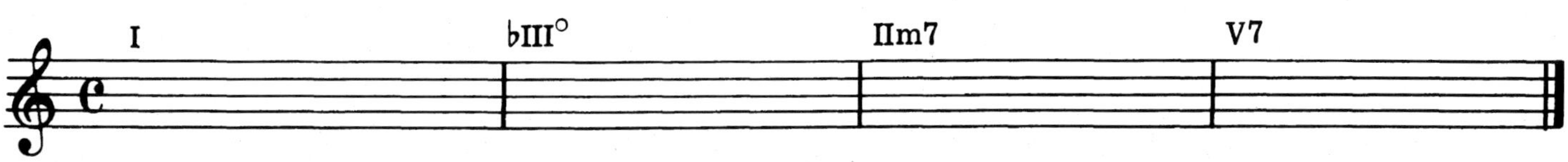

Again

Jazz Scales

We have already looked at several scales that can be used as a springboard for improvisation against certain chords. At this point it will be beneficial to expand our scale vocabulary. Remember, this: There is nothing more dull than to hear a soloist merely run up and down scales when improvising. The important thing is what you do with the scales. I suggest that you keep a notebook and write as many phrases and ideas as you can think of. In addition be sure to play all of your ideas by ear in all keys!

Phrygian Mode

The phrygian mode is another scale that we will study to begin our scale studies on minor type chords. The formula for constructing a phrygian scale is:

Root	- 1/2	- Whole	- Whole	- Whole	- 1/2	- Whole	- Whole
step	step	step	step	step	step	step	step
C	D♭	E♭	F	G	A♭	B♭	C

Phrygian Mode Study

Ear Study

Play the following phrygian scales, both ascending and descending, by ear!

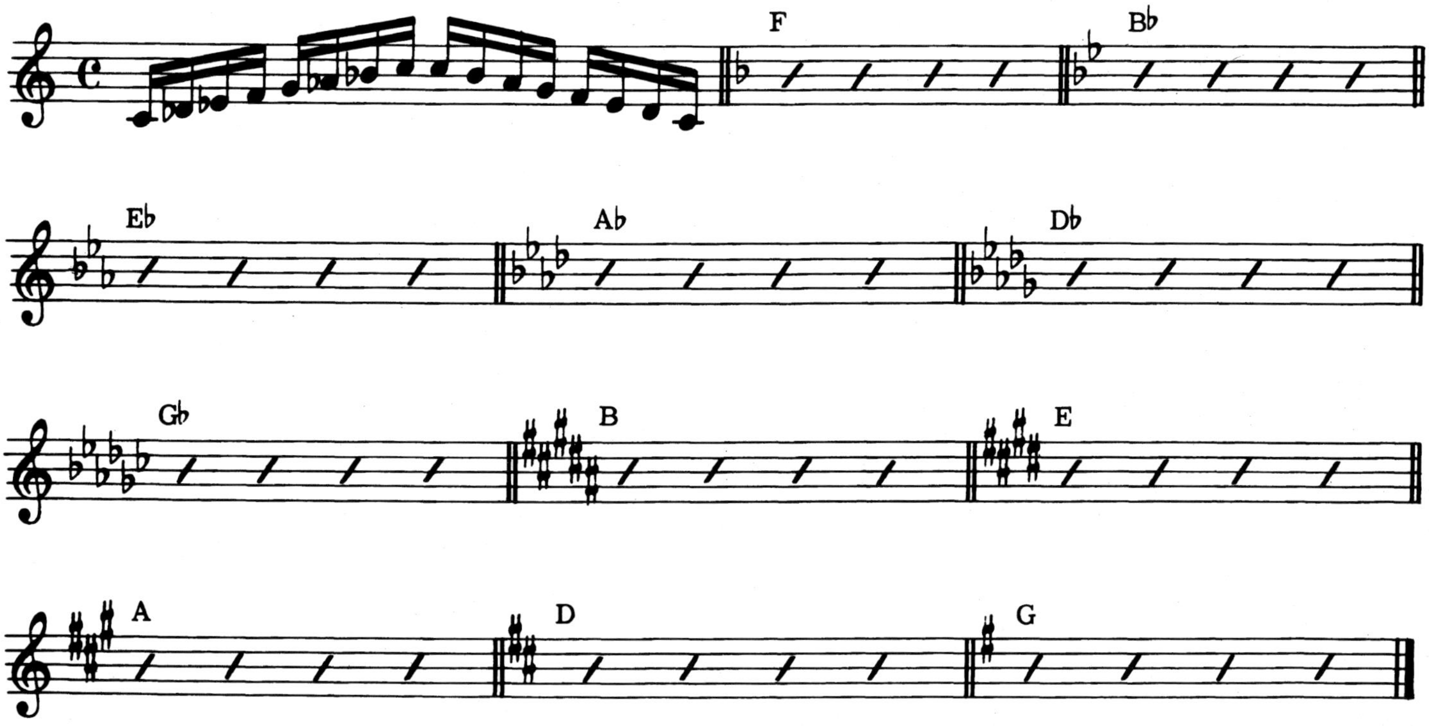

Harmonic Minor

The formula for a harmonic minor scale is:

Root	Whole step	1/2 step	Whole step	Whole step	1/2 step	♭3rd interval	1/2 step
C	E	E♭	F	G	A♭	B♮	C

Harmonic Minor Study

Harmonic Minor Ear Study

Play by ear through the cycle of keys.

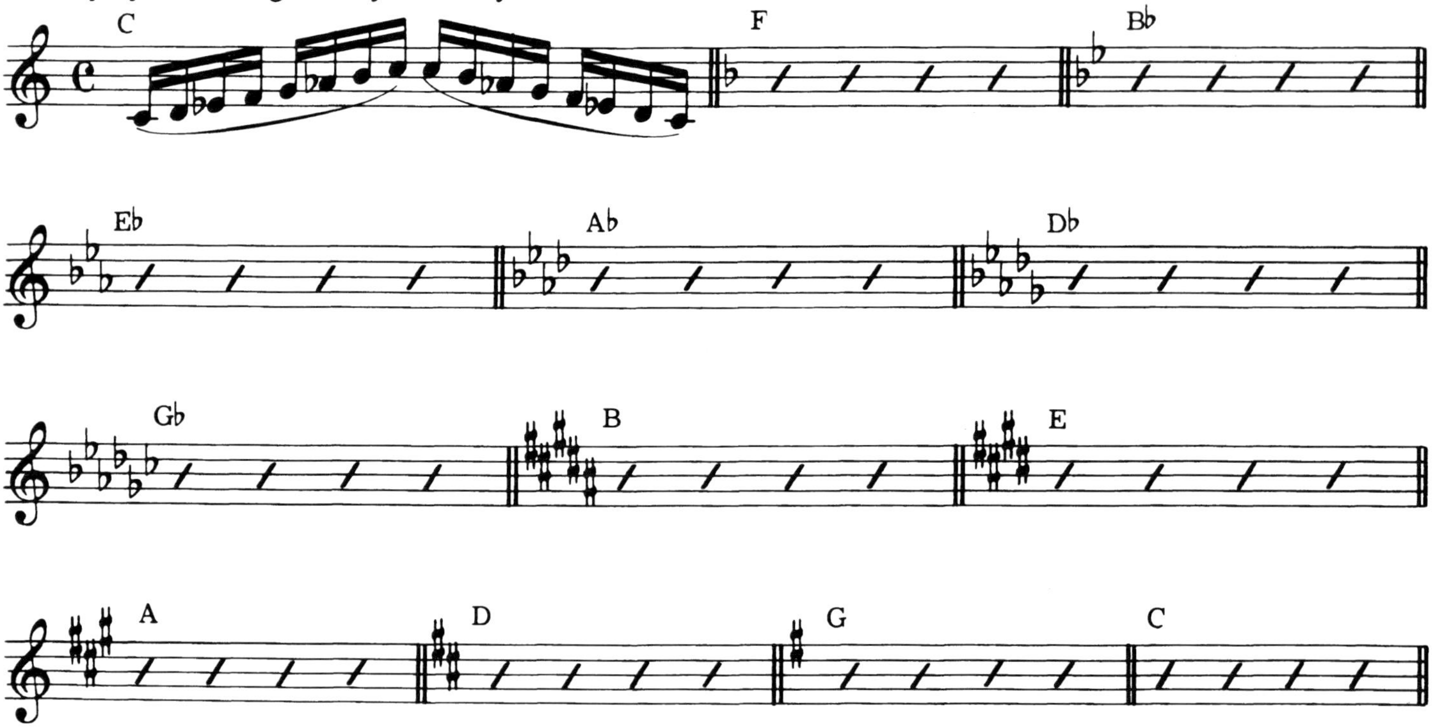

Harmonic to Phrygian

Play by ear through the cycle of keys!
Next, play this study again by ear, only ascend on the phrygian and descend on the harmonic minor.

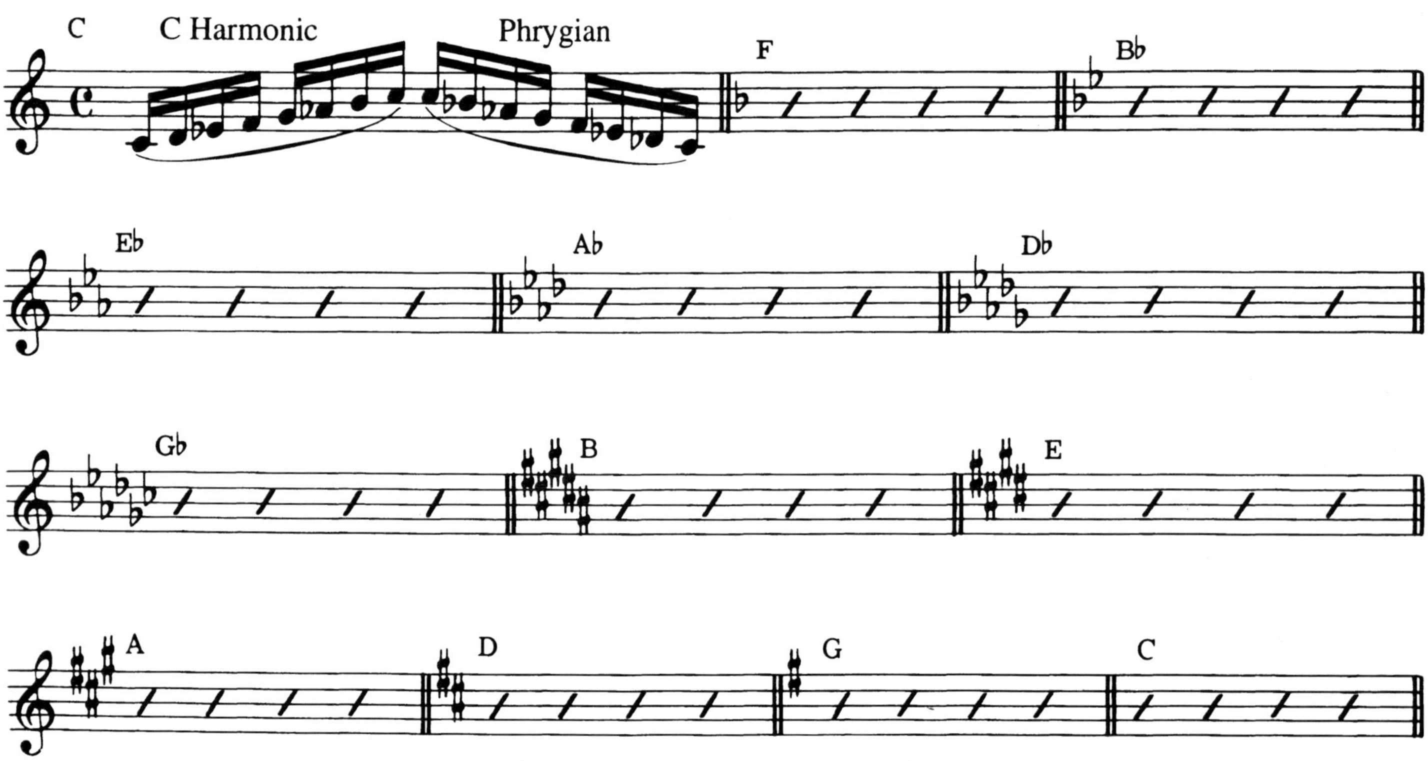

Minor Jazz Scales

Dorian

Formula:
Root - whole - 1/2 - whole - whole - whole - 1/2
step step step step step step

Pure Minor (Aeolian)

Formula: Find relative key-(up minor 3rd)-and begin your scale in that key on the 6th tone of that key. or: R-W-1/2-W-W-1/2-W-W.

Ascending Melodic Minor

Formula:
Root - W - 1/2 - W - W - W - W - 1/2

Harmonic Minor

Formula:
Root - W - 1/2 - W - W - 1/2 - ♭3rd Interval - 1/2

Phrygian

Formula:
Root - 1/2 - W - W - W - 1/2 - W - W

Blues Scale

Formula:
Root - ♭3rd Interval - W - 1/2 - 1/2 - ♭3rd Interval - W

Locrian Scale (Half Diminished)

(Minor Type with ♭5)

Formula:
Root - 1/2 - W - W - 1/2 - W - W - W

Diminished Scale #1

(Begins with Whole Step)

Formula:
Root - W - 1/2 -W - 1/2 - W - 1/2 - W

Several 8, 4 and 2 beat patterns on the minor scales follow.
Play them by ear in all keys. Then, write your own and play them by ear through the keys.

Dorian Studies

1. 

Play by ear in Fm, B♭m, E♭m, A♭m, D♭m, G♭m, Bm, Em, Am, Dm, Gm.

2. 

Play by ear in Fm, B♭m, E♭m, A♭m, D♭m, G♭m, Bm, Em, Am, Dm, Gm.

3. 

Play by ear in Fm, B♭m, E♭m, A♭m, D♭m, G♭m, Bm, Em, Am, Dm, Gm.

4. 

Play by ear in Fm, B♭m, E♭m, A♭m, D♭m, G♭m, Bm, Em, Am, Dm, Gm.

5. 

Play by ear with B♭m7→E♭m7, A♭m7→D♭m7, F♯m7→Bm7, Em7→Am7, Dm7→Gm7.

Aeolian Studies

1. 

Play by ear in Fm, B♭m, E♭m, A♭m, D♭m, G♭m, Bm, Em, Am, Dm, Gm.

2. 

Play by ear in Fm, B♭m, E♭m, A♭m, D♭m, G♭m, Bm, Em, Am, Dm, Gm,

3. 

Play by ear in Fm, B♭m, E♭m, A♭m, D♭m, G♭m, Bm, Em, Am, Dm, Gm.

4. 

Play by ear in Fm, B♭m, E♭m, A♭m, D♭m, G♭m, Bm, Em, Am, Dm, Gm.

5. 

Play by ear with B♭m7→E♭m7, A♭m7→D♭m7, F♯m7→Bm7, Em7→Am7, Dm7→Gm7.

Ascending Melodic Studies

1.

Play by ear in Fm, B♭m, E♭m, A♭m, D♭m, G♭m, Bm, Em, Am, Dm, Gm.

2.

Play by ear in Fm, B♭m, E♭m, A♭m, D♭m, G♭m, Bm, Em, Am, Dm, Gm.

3.

Play by ear in Fm, B♭m, E♭m, A♭m, D♭m, G♭m, Bm, Em, Am, Dm, Gm.

4.

Play by ear in Fm, B♭m, E♭m, A♭m, D♭m, G♭m, Bm, Em, Am, Dm, Gm.

5.

Play by ear with B♭m → E♭m, A♭m → D♭m, F♯m → Bm, Em → Am, Dm → Gm.

Harmonic Minor Studies

1.

Play by ear in Fm, B♭m, E♭m, A♭m, D♭m, G♭m, Bm, Em, Am, Dm, Gm.

2.

Play by ear in Fm, B♭m, E♭m, A♭m, D♭m, G♭m, Bm, Em, Am, Dm, Gm.

3.

Play by ear in Fm, B♭m, E♭m, A♭m, D♭m, G♭m, Bm, Em, Am, Dm, Gm.

4.

Play by ear in Fm, B♭m, E♭m, A♭m, D♭m, G♭m, Bm, Em, Am, Dm, Gm.

5.

Play by ear with B♭m → E♭m, A♭m → D♭m, F♯m → Bm Em → Am, Dm → Gm.

Phrygian Studies

1. 

Play by ear in Fm, B♭m, E♭m, A♭m, D♭m, G♭m, Bm, Em, Am, Dm, Gm.

2. 

Play by ear in Fm, B♭m, E♭m, A♭m, D♭m, G♭m, Bm, Em, Am, Dm, Gm.

3. 

Play by ear in Fm, B♭m, E♭m, A♭m, D♭m, G♭m, Bm, Em, Am, Dm, Gm.

4. 

Play by ear in Fm, B♭m, E♭m, A♭m, D♭m, G♭m, Bm, Em, Am, Dm, Gm.

5. 

Play by ear with B♭m→E♭m, A♭m→D♭m, F♯m→Bm, Em→Am, Dm→Gm.

Blues Scale Studies

1. 

Play by ear in Fm, B♭m, E♭m, A♭m, D♭m, G♭m, Bm, Em, Am, Dm, Gm.

2. 

Play by ear in Fm, B♭m, E♭m, A♭m, D♭m, G♭m, Bm, Em, Am, Dm, Gm.

3. 

Play by ear in Fm, B♭m, E♭m, A♭m, D♭m, G♭m, Bm, Em, Am, Dm, Gm.

4. 

Play by ear in Fm, B♭m, E♭m, A♭m, D♭m, G♭m, Bm, Em, Am, Dm, Gm,

5. 

Play by ear with B♭m→E♭m, A♭m→D♭m, F♯m→Bm, Em→Am, Dm→Gm.

Locrian Studies

(Half Diminished)

1. 

Play by ear in Fm, Bbm, Ebm, Abm, Dbm, Gbm, Bm, Em, Am, Dm, Gm.

2. 

Play by ear in Fm, Bbm, Ebm, Abm, Dbm, Gbm, Bm, Em, Am, Dm, Gm.

3. 

Play by ear in Fm, Bbm, Ebm, Abm, Dbm, Gbm, Bm, Em, Am, Dm, Gm.

4. 

Play by ear in Fm, Bbm, Ebm, Abm, Dbm, Gbm, Bm, Em, Am, Dm, Gm.

5. 

Play by ear with Bbm-5 → Ebm-5, Abm-5 → Dbm-5, F♯m-5 → Bm-5, Em-5 → Am-5, Dm-5 → Gm-5.

Diminished #1 Studies

1. 

Play by ear in Fm, Bbm, Ebm, Abm, Dbm, Gbm, Bm, Em, Am, Dm, Gm.

2. 

Play by ear in Fm, Bbm, Ebm, Abm, Dbm, Gbm, Bm, Em, Am, Dm, Gm.

3. 

Play by ear in Fm, Bbm, Ebm, Abm, Dbm, Gbm, Bm, Em, Am, Dm, Gm.

4. 

Play by ear in Fm, Bbm, Ebm, Abm, Dbm, Gbm, Bm, Em, Am, Dm, Gm.

5. 

Play by ear with Bbm → Ebm, Abm → Dbm, F♯m → Bm, Em → Am, Dm → Gm.

Direct Substitution

When major chords appear, you may substitute the following chords. (Your ear should tell you which chords fit well and which ones do not work as well in a given situation.)

For a Major Chord: Use major 7th, major 6th, major 9th, 6th add9.

Write and Play

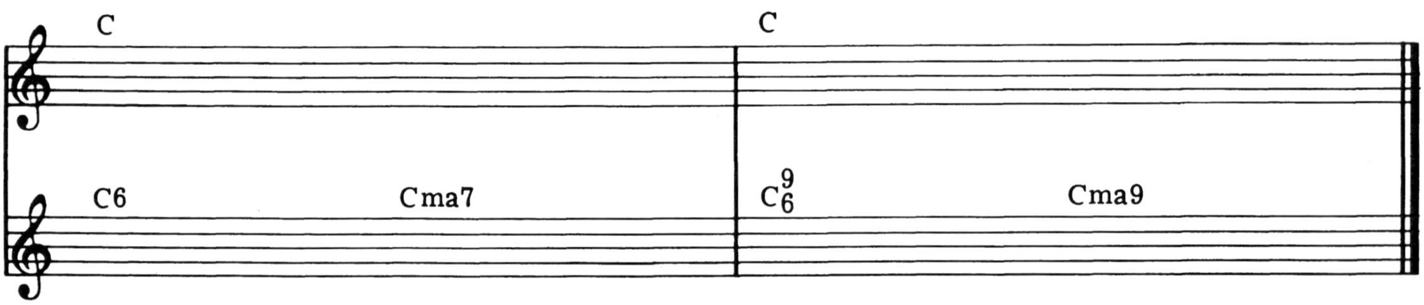

When minor chords appear, you may substitute the following chords. (Your ear should decide which substitution works best.)

For a Minor Chord: Use minor 6th, minor 7th, minor 9th, major 7♭3, minor 6th add 9.

Write and Play

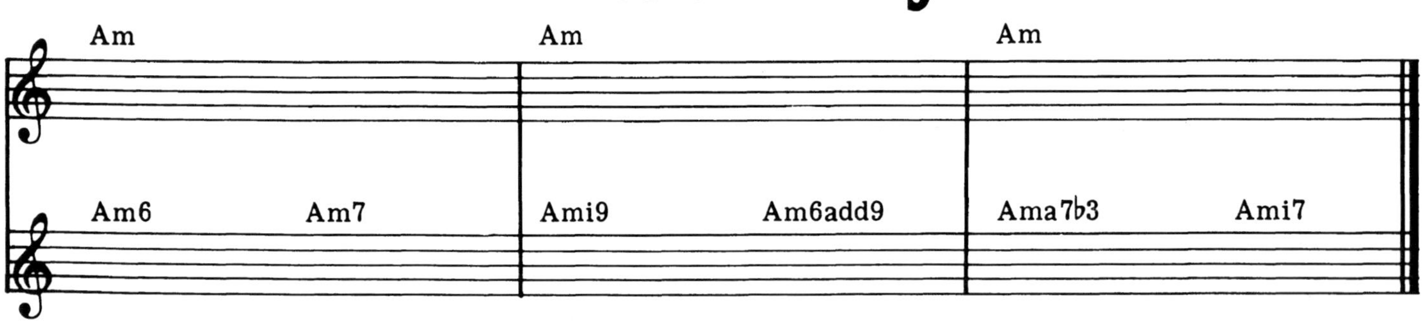

Improvisation Study

(Play Appropriate Scale Ideas with the Following Chords)

Improvising Study #2

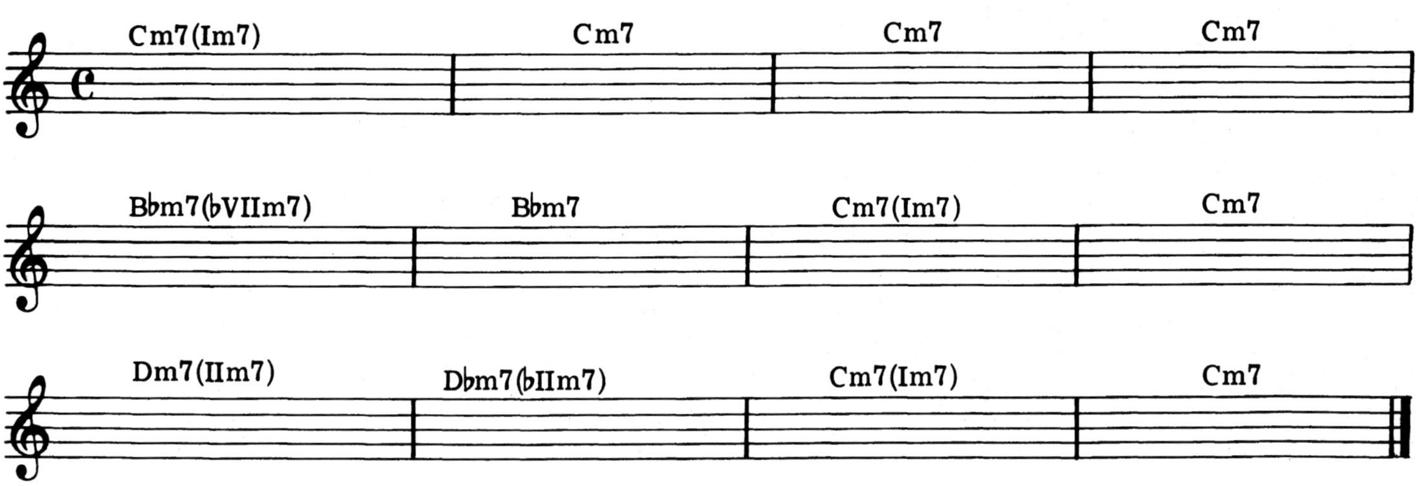

Play the above progression-using your Improvising Ideas — in the keys of Fm, B♭m, E♭m, A♭m, D♭m, G♭m, Bm, Em, Am, Dm, Gm.

I-VIm-IIm-V7-I

Bossa nova

Play the above studies by ear in F, B♭, E♭, A♭, D♭, G♭, B, E, A, D, G.

Write Your Own and Play in All Keys

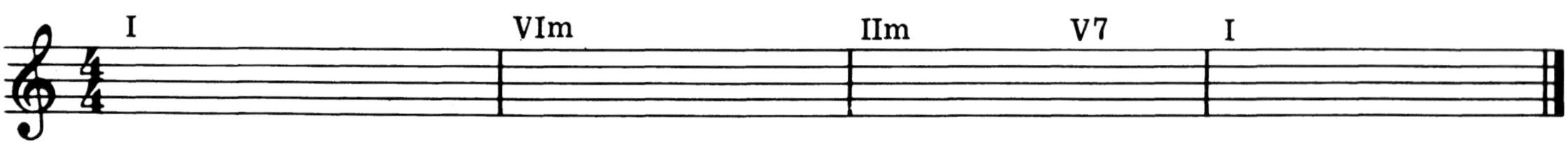

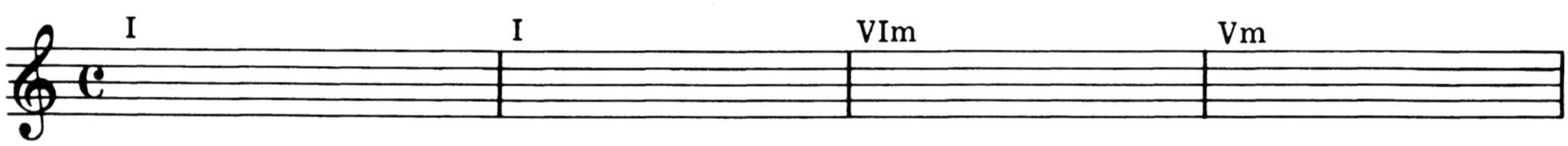

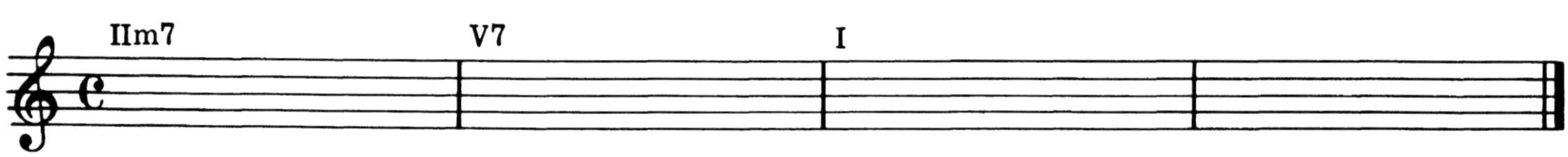

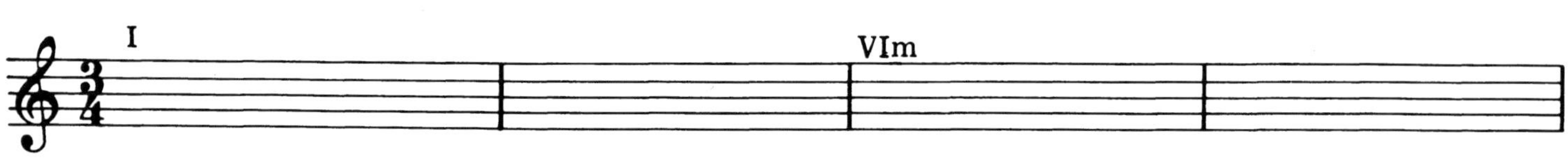

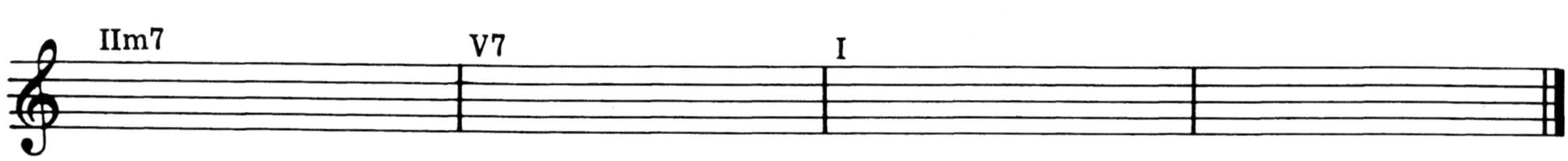

I-IIIm-IIm-V7-I

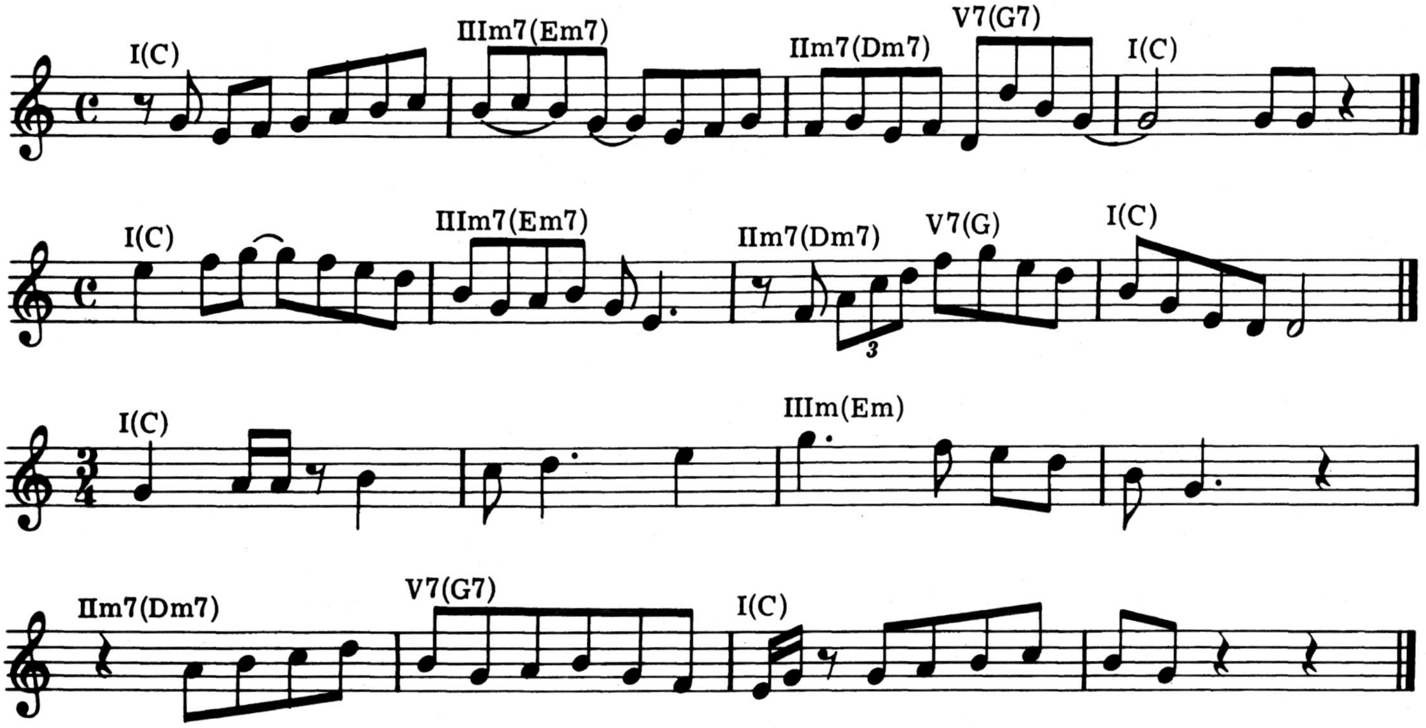

Play the above examples by ear in F, B♭, E♭, A♭, D♭, G♭, B, E, A, D, G.

Write your own examples and play them by ear in all keys. Remember to use substitute chords as explained on page 107.

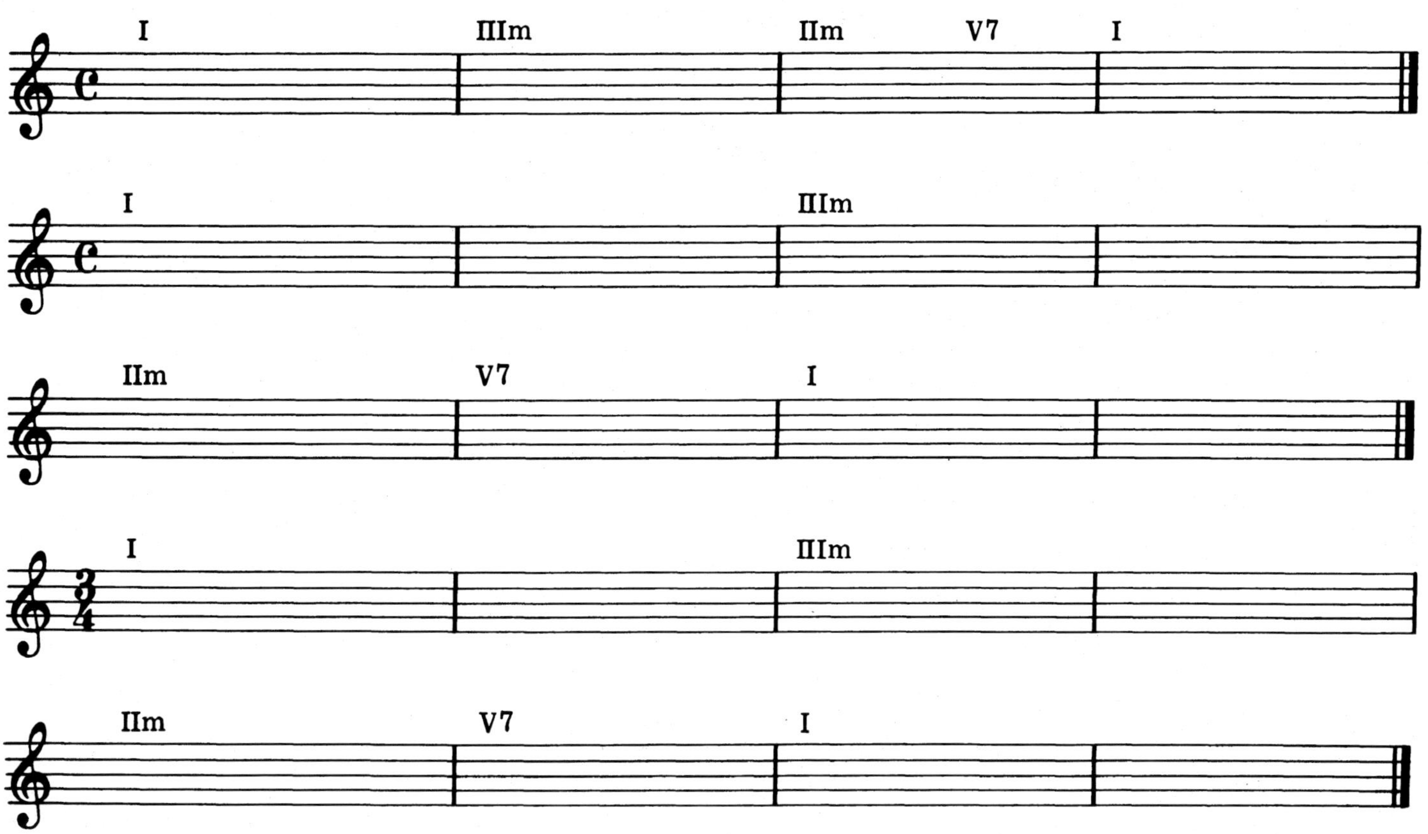

I-Vm6-IV-VI7-IIm7-V7-I

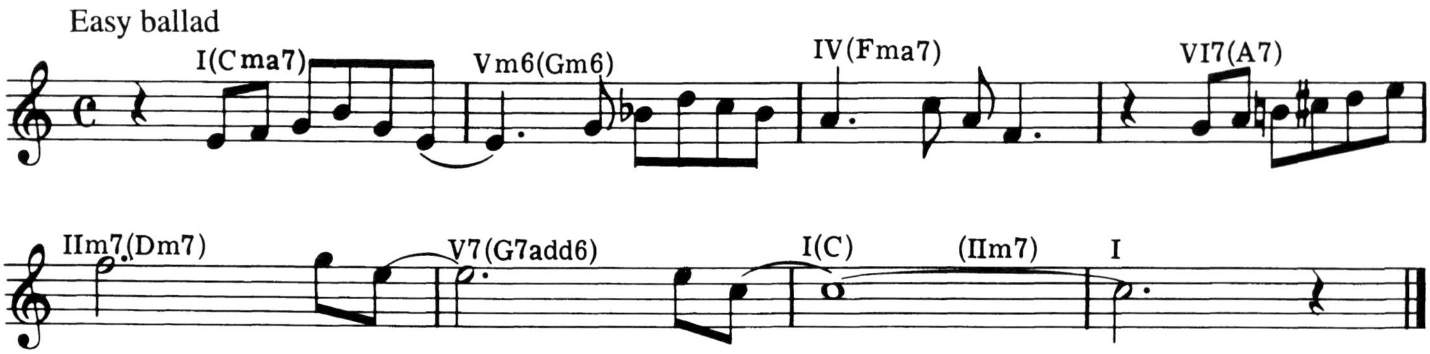

Write Your Own and Play in All Keys

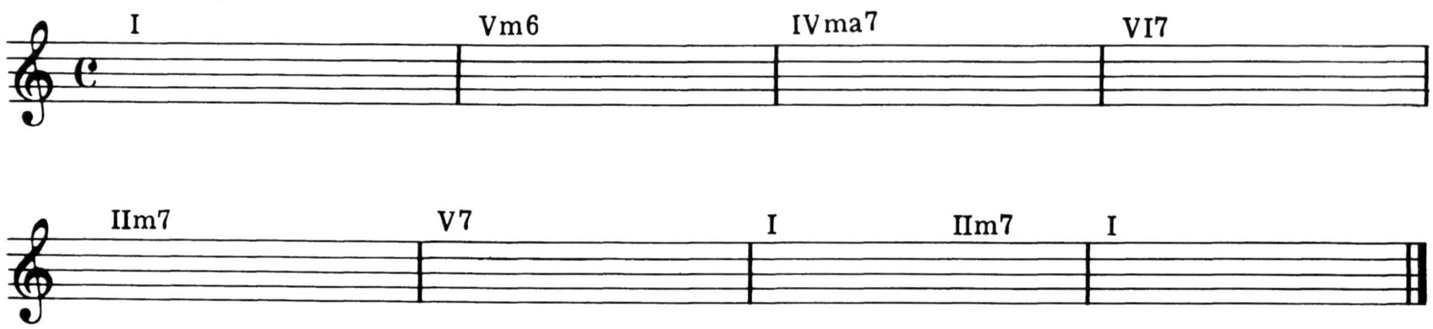

Write Another

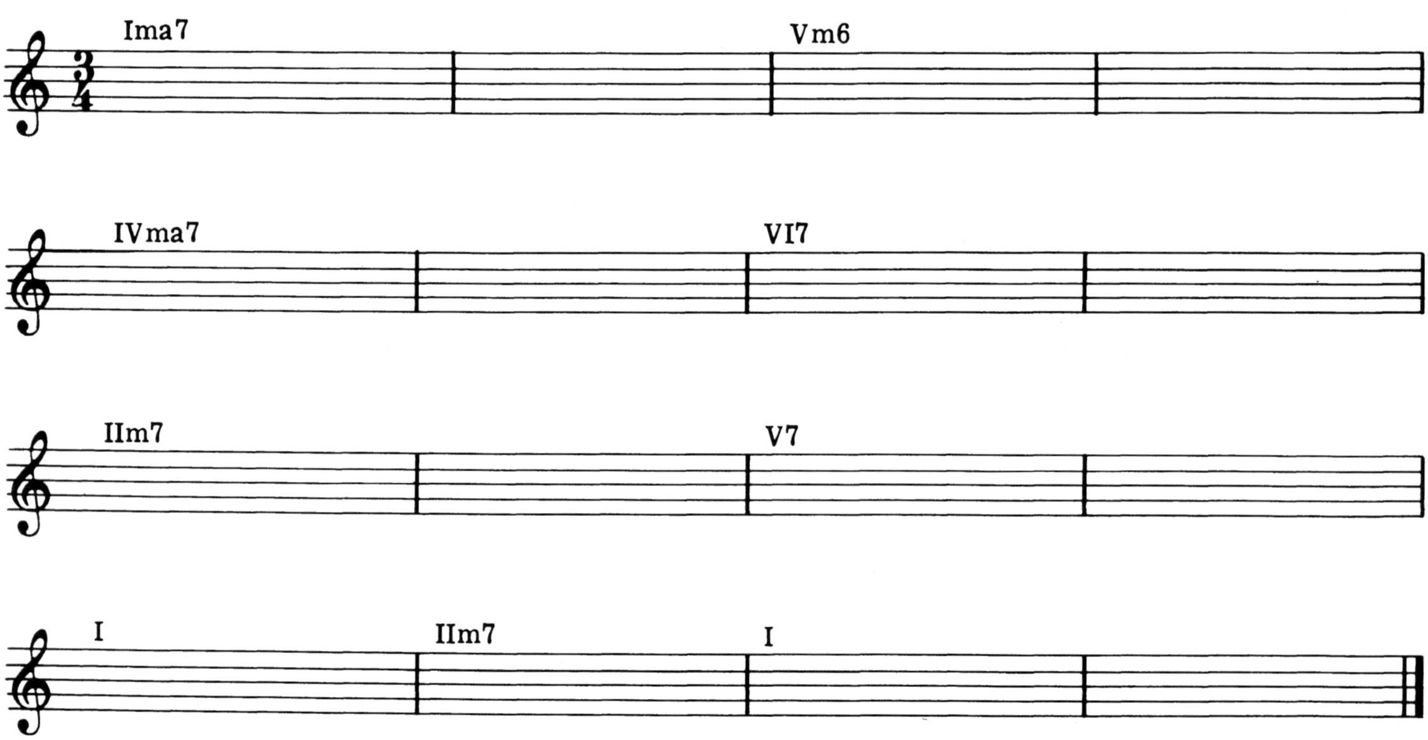

Whole Tone Scale

The whole tone scale may be used against any dominant 7th type of chord with a ♯5 or a ♭5.

The formula for building a whole tone scale is:

Root	Whole step	Whole step	Whole step	Whole step	Whole step	Whole step
C	D	E	F♯	G♯	B♭	C

Write, play, and sing the following whole tone scales.

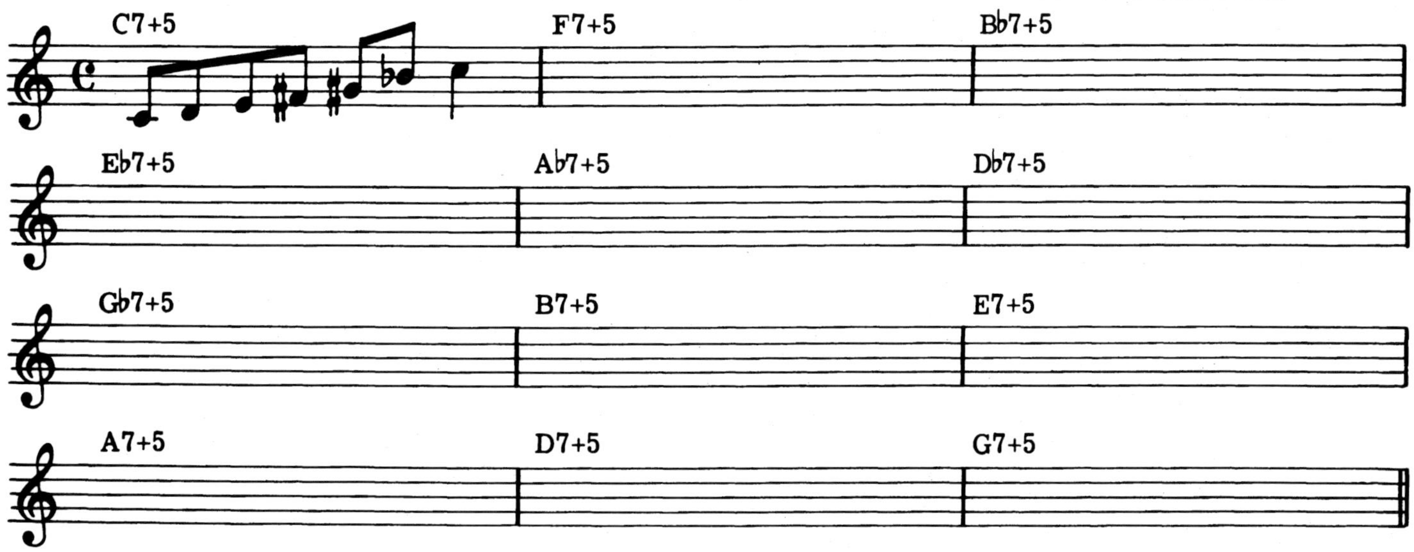

Whole Tone Scales

1. 

Play by ear in F, B♭, E♭, A♭, D♭, G♭, B, E, A, D, G.

2. 

Play by ear in F, B♭, E♭, A♭, D♭, G♭, B, E, A, D, G.

3. 

Play by ear in F, B♭, E♭, A♭, D♭, G♭, B, E, A, D, G.

4. 

Play by ear in F, B♭, E♭, A♭, D♭, G♭, B, E, A, D, G.

5. 

Play by ear with B♭+ → E♭+, A♭+ → D♭+, F♯+ → B+, E+ → A+, D+ → G+.

6. 

Play by ear with B♭+ → E♭+, A♭+ → D♭+, F♯+ → B+, E+ → A+, D+ → G+.

Diminished Scale #2

On page 110 we studied the diminished scale #1. Diminished scale #1 began with a whole step.
1 relates directly to the diminished chord and can be used as a substitute scale against minor chords. Diminished scale #2 begins with a 1/2 step interval. The formula for constructing diminished scale #2 is:

Root	1/2 step	Whole step	1/2 step	Whole step	1/2 step	Whole step	1/2 step	Whole step
C	D♭	E♭	E♮	F♯	G	A	B♭	C

These chord types: (7-5, 7♭9, 7+9, 7♭9+11, 7♯9, 7♯9♯11)

Construct the Following #2 Dim. Scales

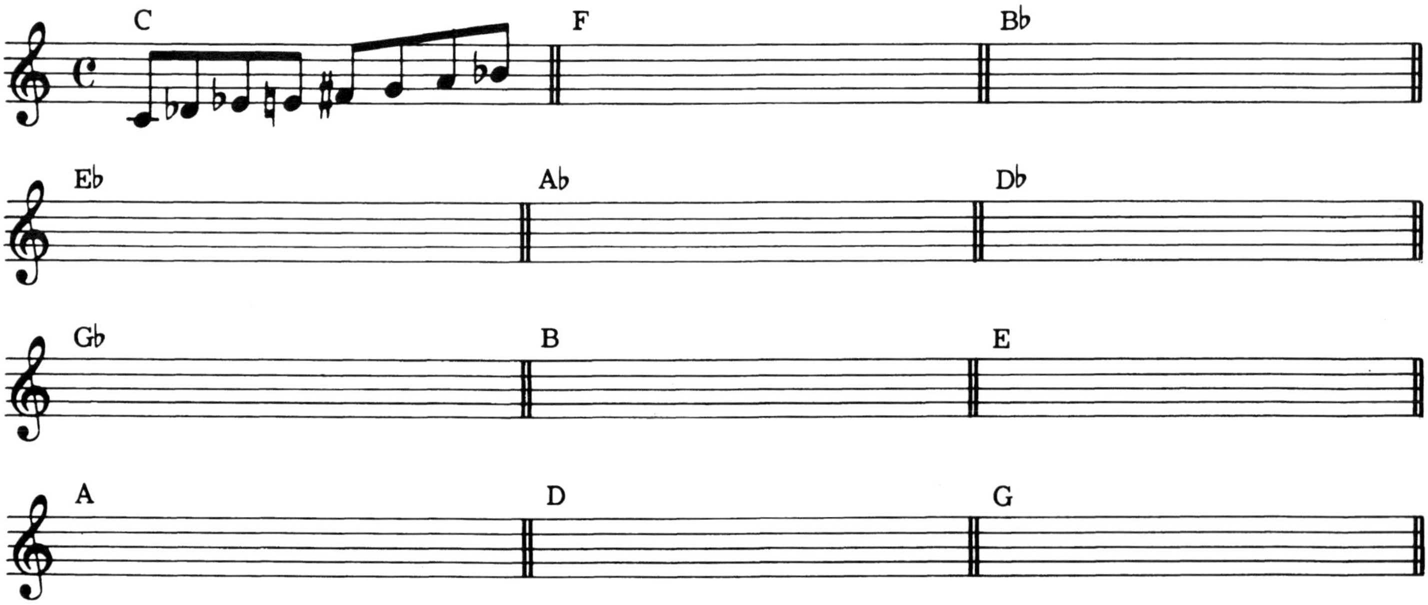

Diminished Scale #2 Studies

1.  Play by ear in F, B♭, E♭, A♭, D♭, G♭, B, E, A, D, G.

2. 

Play by ear in F, B♭, E♭, A♭, D♭, G♭, B, E, A, D, G.

3. 

Play by ear in F, B♭, E♭, A♭, D♭, G♭, B, E, A, D, G.

4. 

Play by ear with B♭+11→ E♭+11, A♭+11→ D♭+11, F♯11→ B+11
E+11→ A+11, D+11→ G+11

5. 

Play by ear with B♭+11→ E♭+11, A♭+11→ D♭+11, F♯+11→ B+11
E+11→ A+11, D+11→ G+11.

Turn Arounds and Endings

At the end of a song, rhythm player's frequently add a 2 bar phrase to lead back into the beginning. This is done to relieve the monotony of playing the I chord for several measures. Below are some common turn arounds. Play them in all keys!

Write Your Own and Play in All Keys!

1.

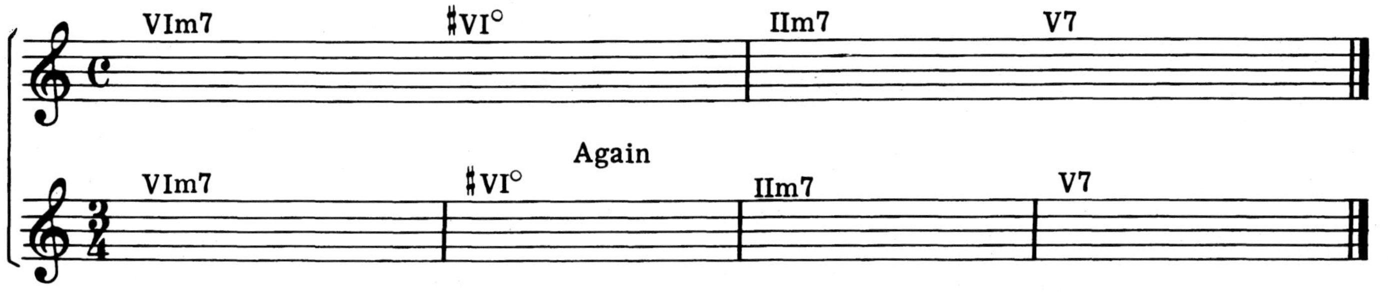

2.

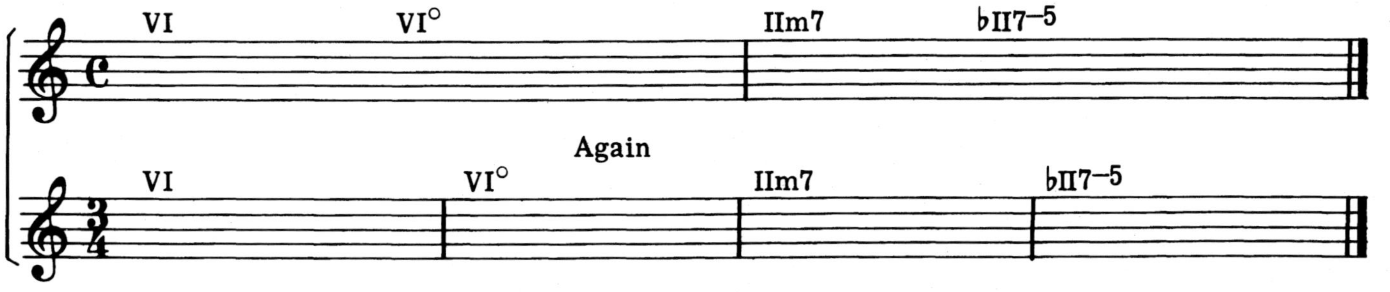

3.

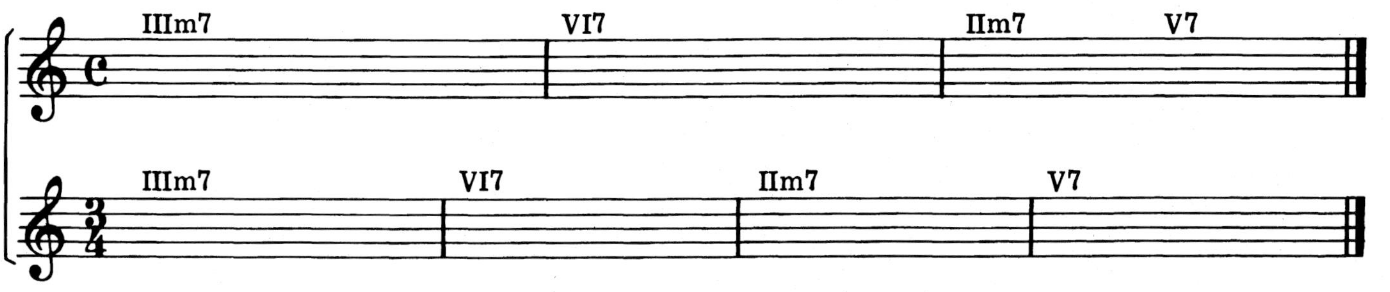

4.

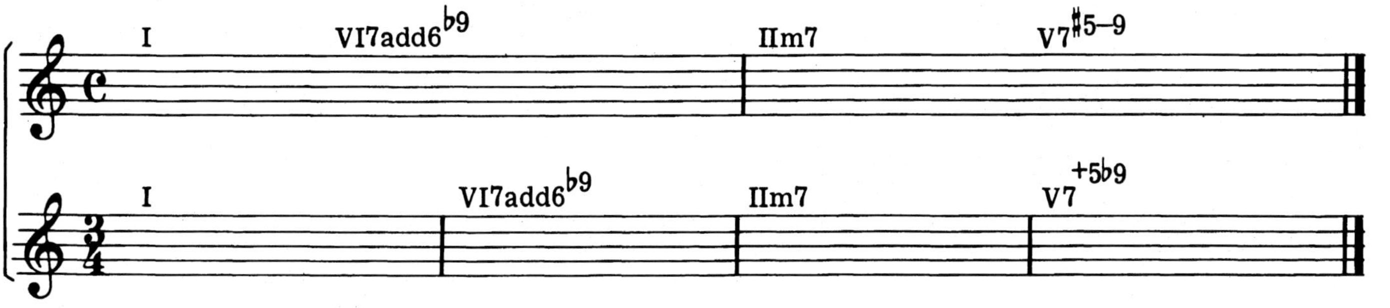

5.

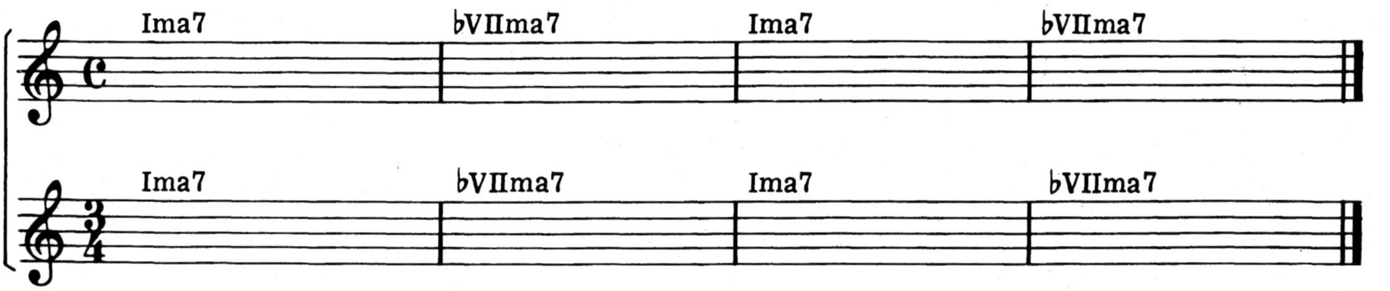

Bridges

The middle section or "B" section of tunes is called "the bridge". Some fairly typical bridges are presented on the following pages. Write solos and experiment by playing them by ear **in all keys!**

1

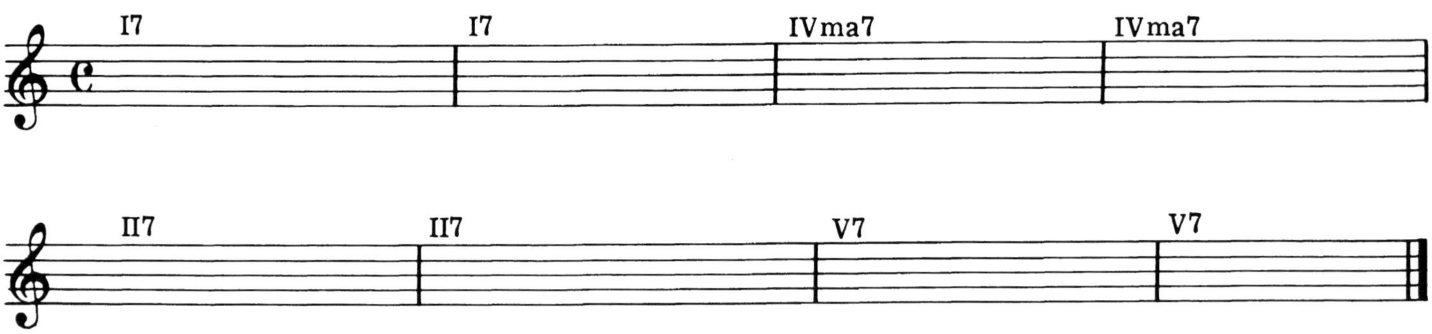

2

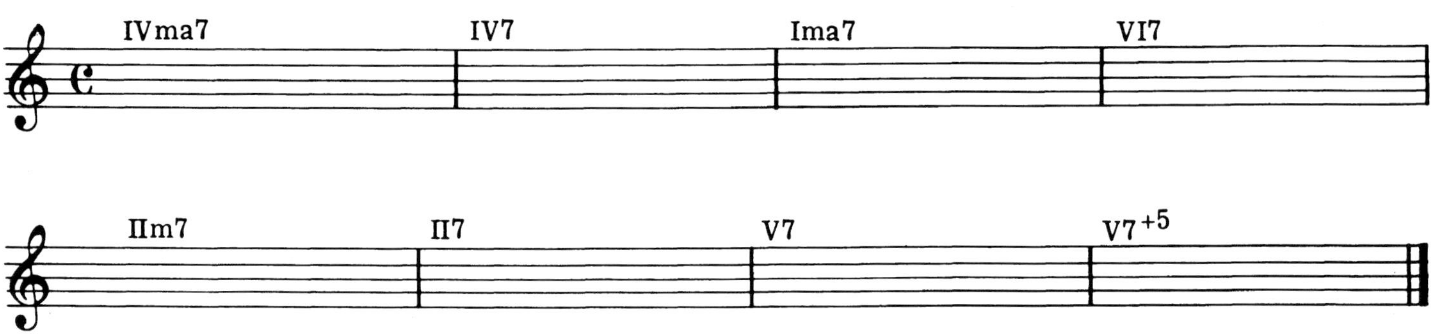

3

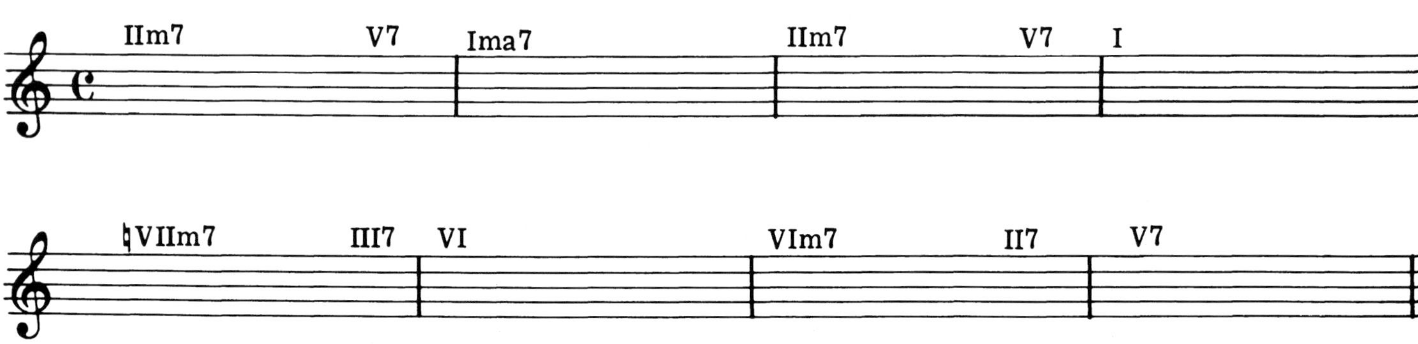

4

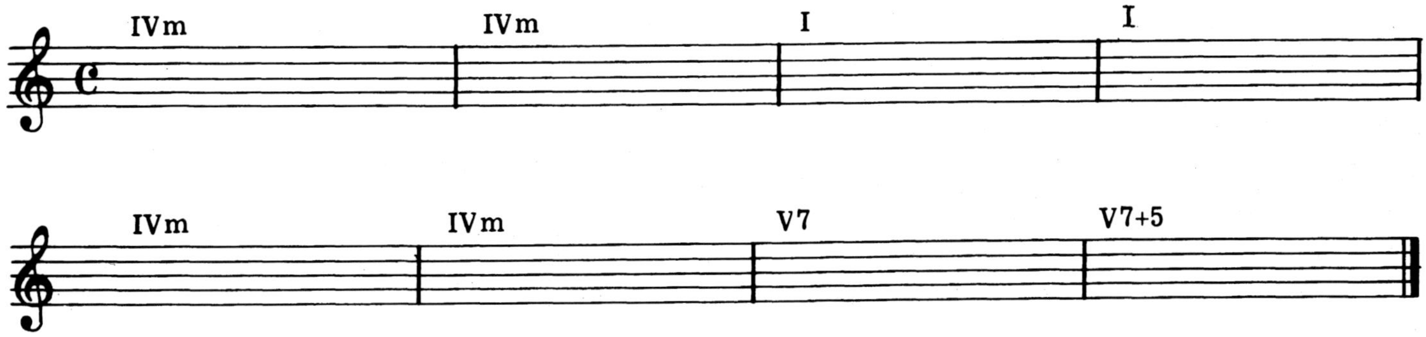
IVm IVm I I
IVm IVm V7 V7+5

5

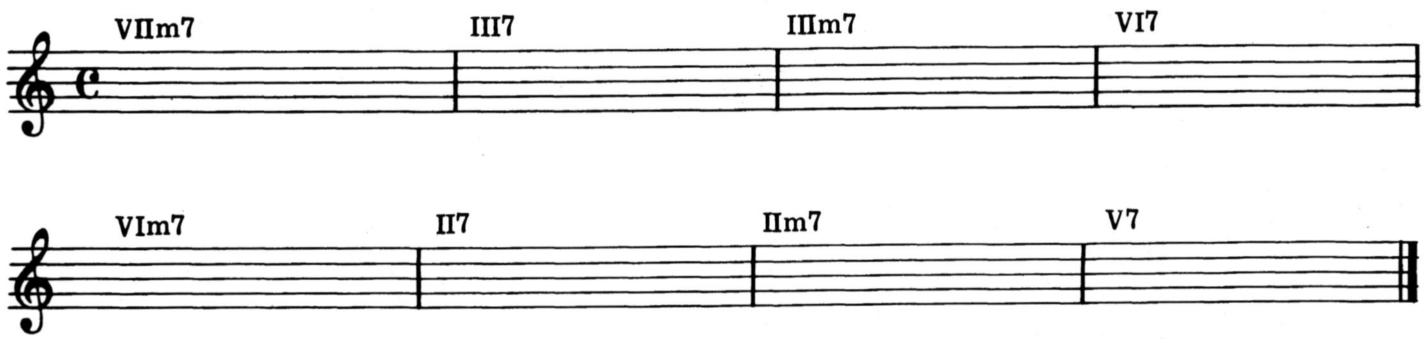
VIIm7 III7 IIIm7 VI7
VIm7 II7 IIm7 V7

6

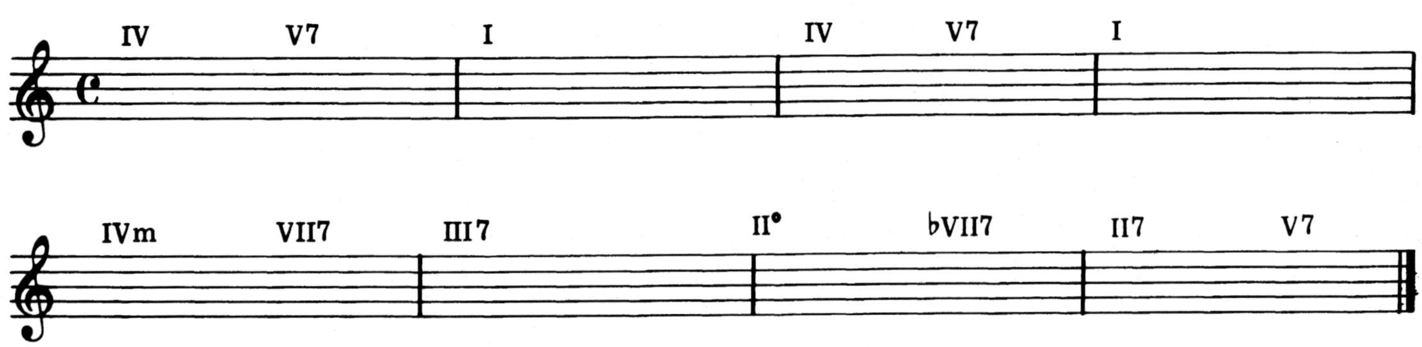
IV V7 I IV V7 I
IVm VII7 III7 II° ♭VII7 II7 V7

7

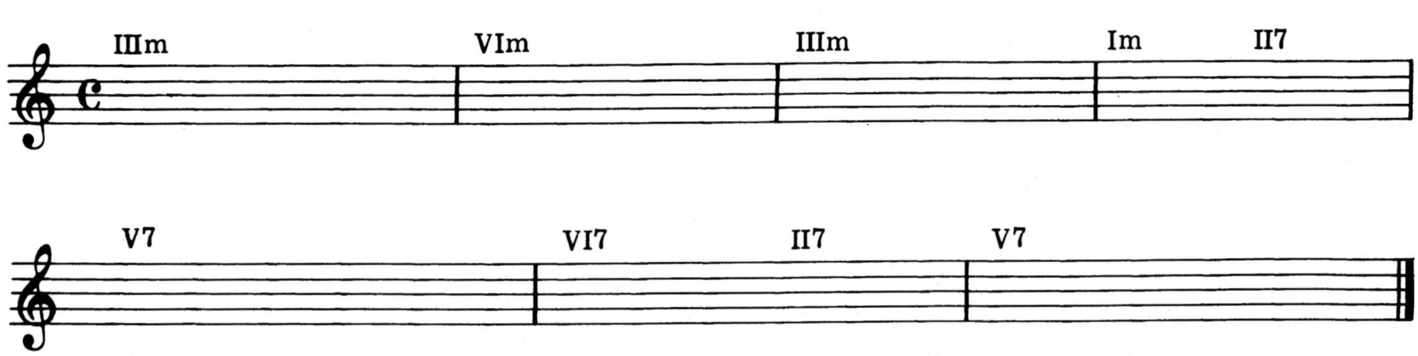
IIIm VIm IIIm Im II7
V7 VI7 II7 V7

8

Notice the chromatic motion in this bridge.

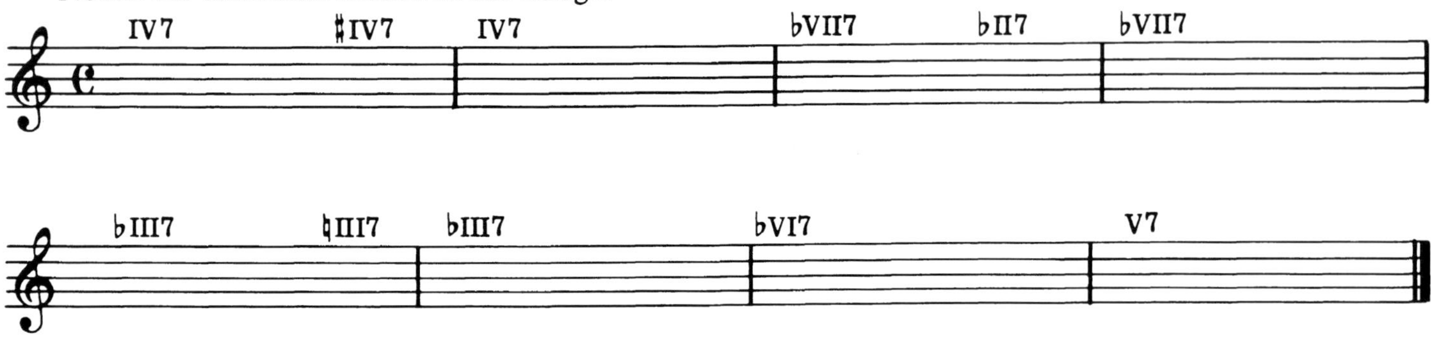

9

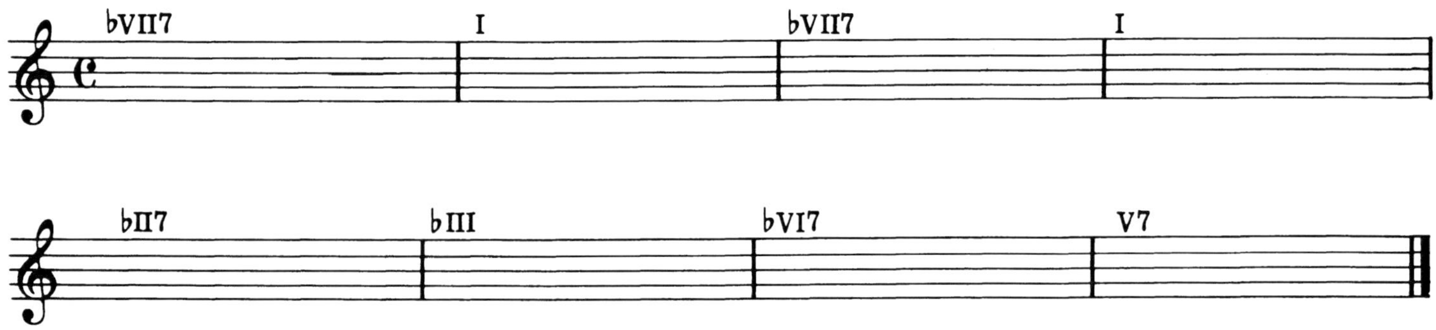

10

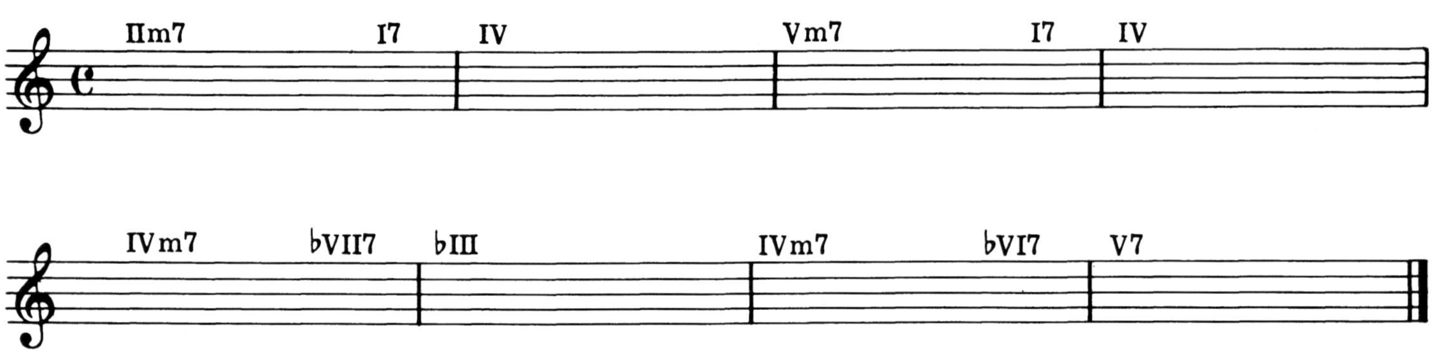

11

12

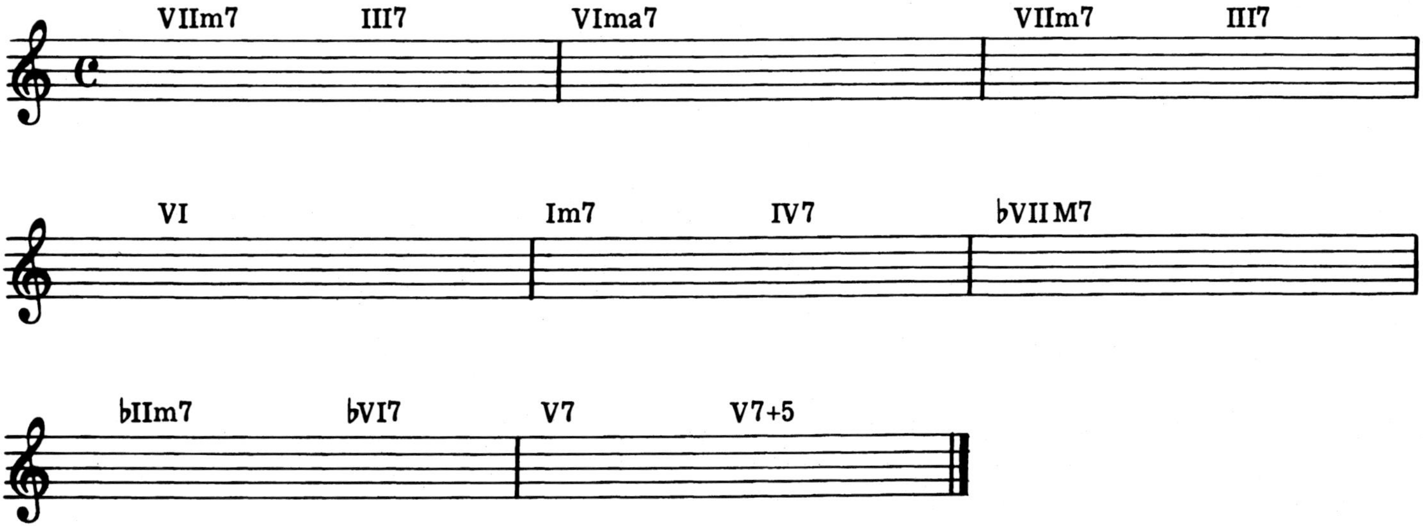
VIIm7
III7
VIma7
VIIm7
III7
VI
Im7
IV7
♭VII M7
♭IIm7
♭VI7
V7
V7+5

13

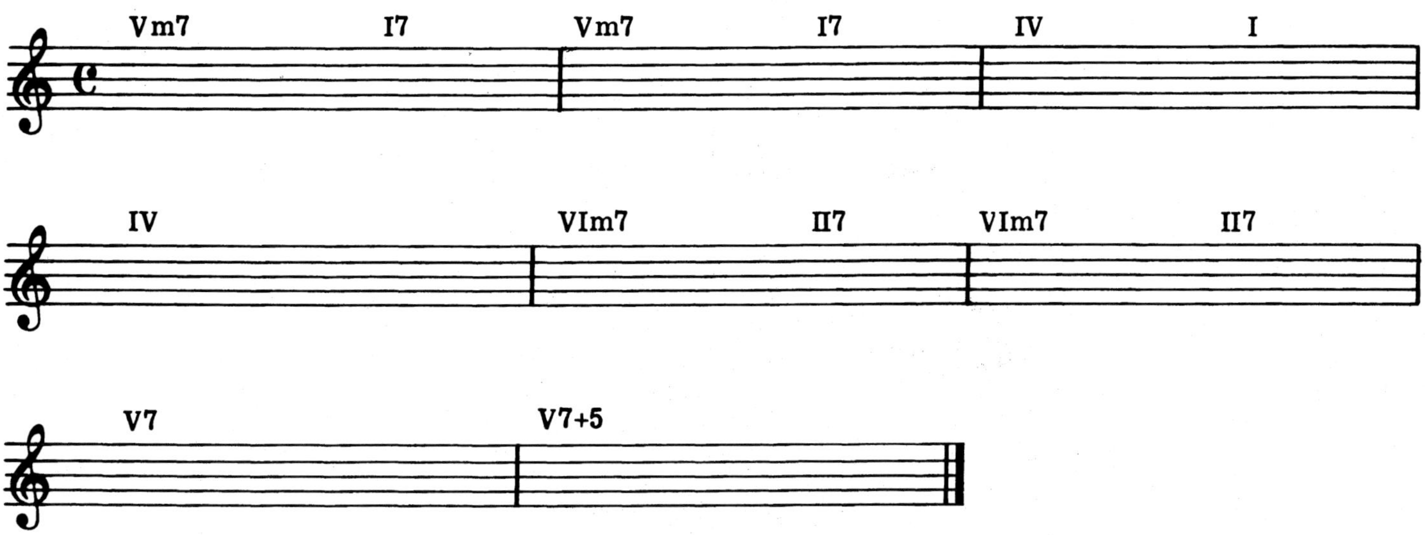
Vm7
I7
Vm7
I7
IV
I
IV
VIm7
II7
VIm7
II7
V7
V7+5

14

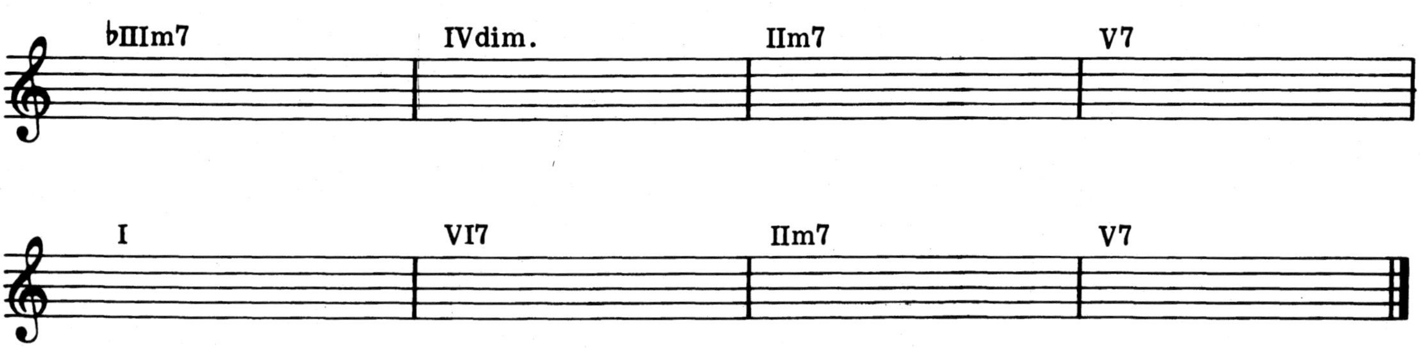
♭IIIm7
IVdim.
IIm7
V7
I
VI7
IIm7
V7

More Blues

We are now ready to play more blues changes. Before proceeding, review pages 87, 88 and 118 on the blues scale.
The basic blues progression is I7 (4 measure)
IV7 (2 measure)
I7 (2 measure)
V7 (2 measure)
I7 (2 measure)

Shuffle tempo

Write your own choruses - Play the chord changes - And transpose your ideas into all keys by ear!

Your Blues

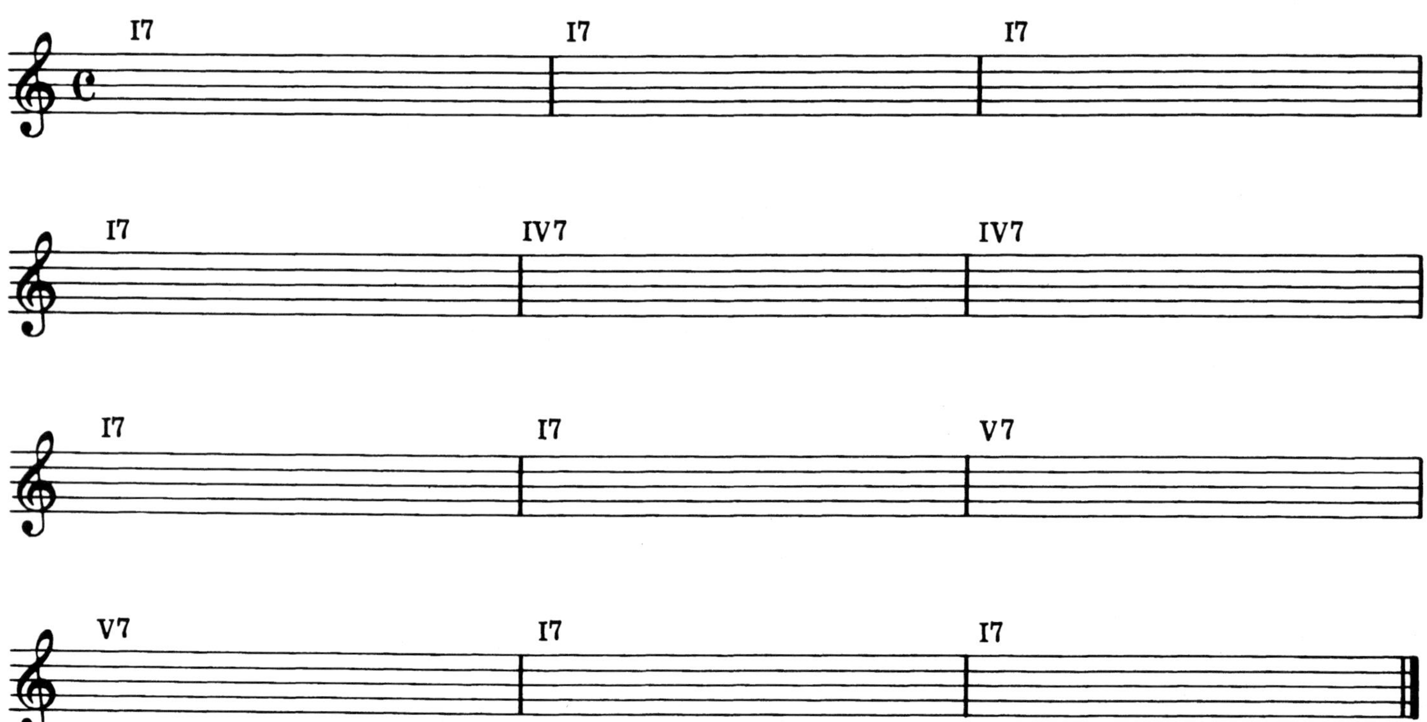

Another Blues

(Write and Play in All Keys!)

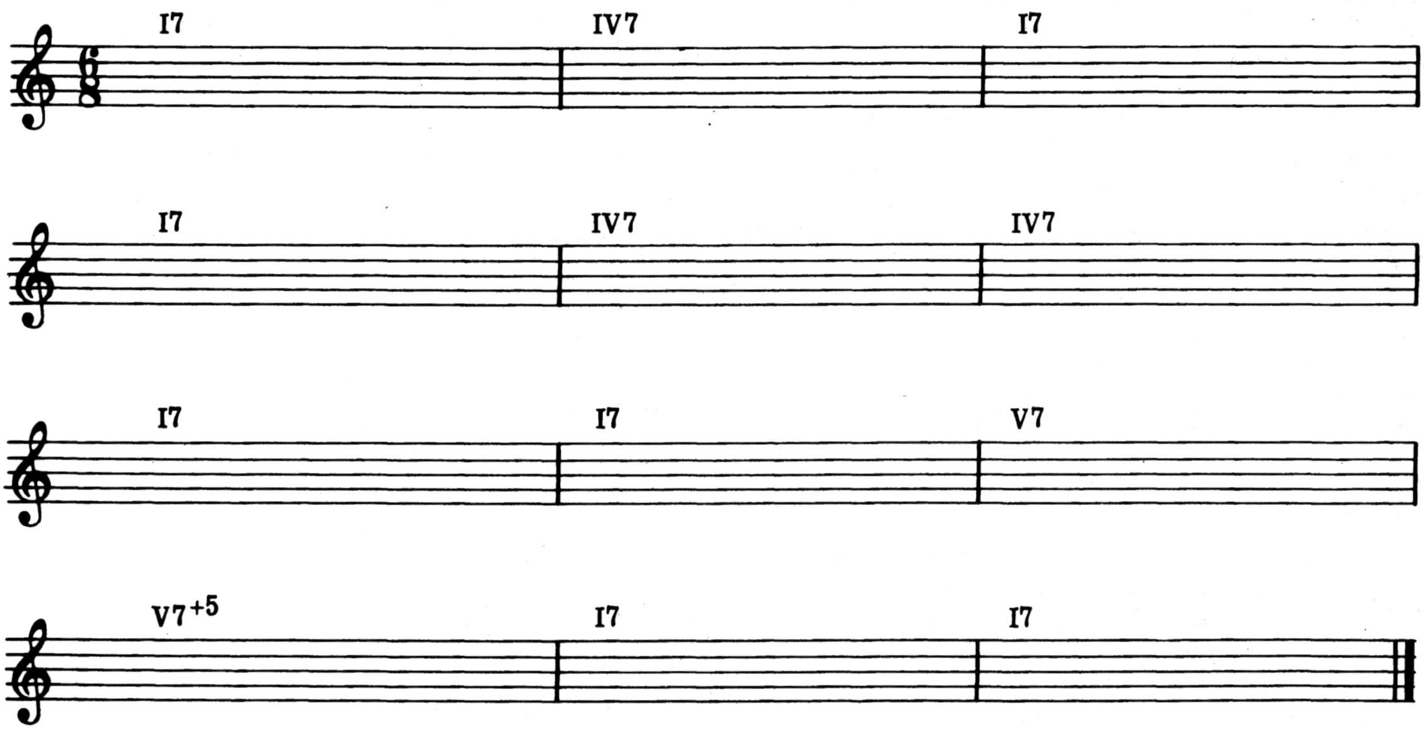

Alternate Blues Changes

Frequently, the basic blues changes are slightly altered. Below are several such typical alterations. Play through the changes, play a chorus or two by ear, write new ideas, and play them by ear in all keys.

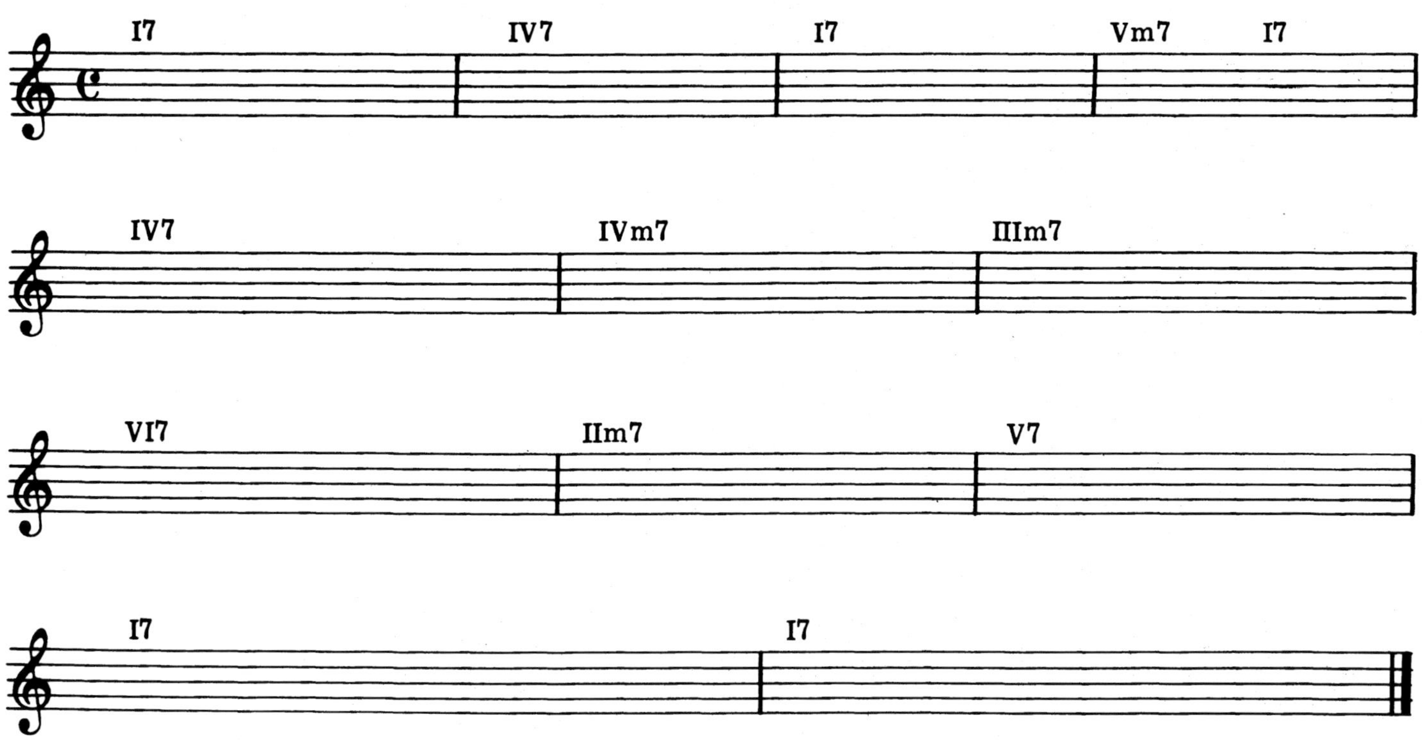

Minor Blues

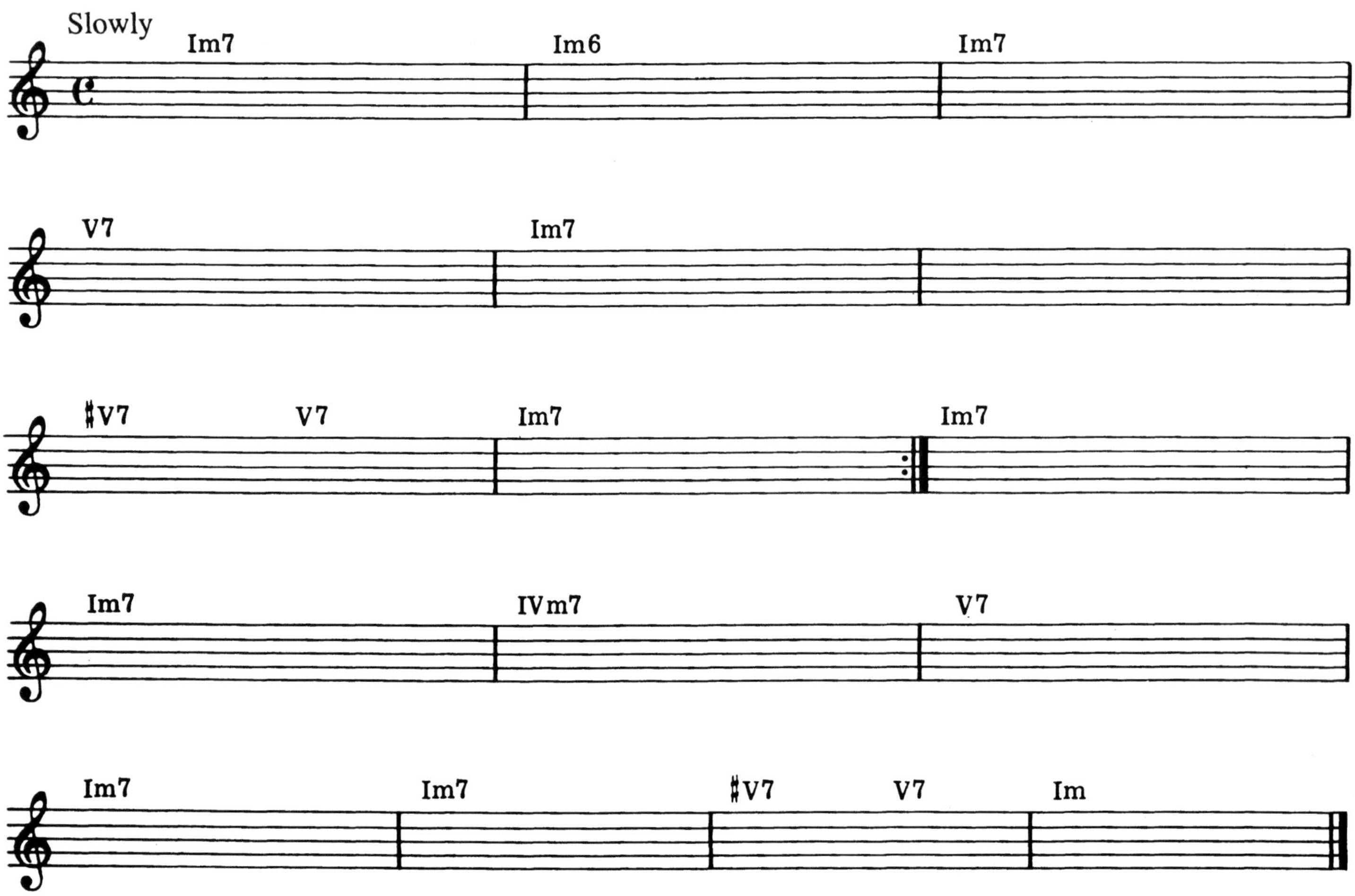

Another Minor Blues

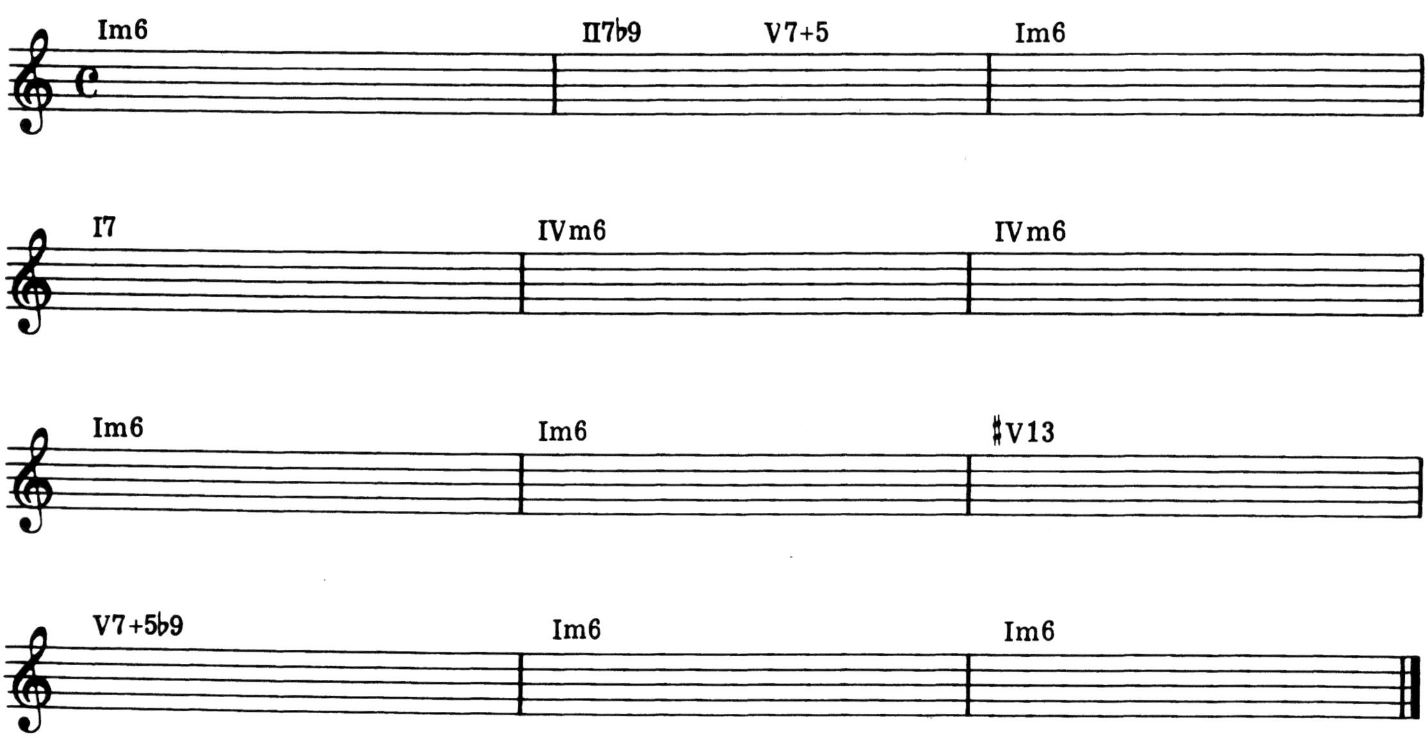

Expanding Improvisational Ideas

We have up to now been looking at improvisation in a linear fashion. We can begin to see the expanding range of improvisational possibilities if we look at the various scales harmonized in triads. That is to say, if we build triads (3 note chords) on each note of a scale and use only tones in that scale, we have arrived at other chord possibilities.
We will consider 4 types of triads:

Major Triad

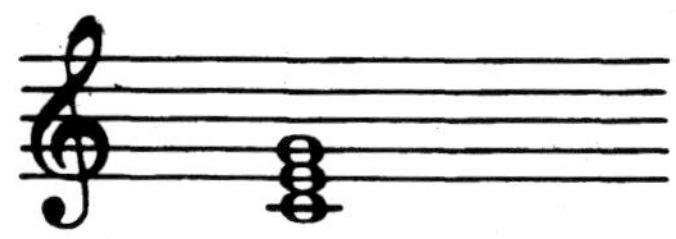

Formula: Root - 3rd - 5th
(Root–3rd: Major 3rd Interval; 3rd–5th: Minor 3rd Interval)

Minor Triad

Formula: Root - ♭3rd - 5th
(Root–♭3rd: Minor 3rd Interval; ♭3rd–5th: Major 3rd Interval)

Augmented Triad

Formula: Root - 3rd - ♯5th
(Root–3rd: Major 3rd Interval; 3rd–♯5th: Major 3rd Interval)

Diminished Triad

Formula: Root - ♭3rd - ♭5th
(Root–♭3rd: Minor 3rd Interval; ♭3rd–♭5th: Minor 3rd Interval)

Major Scale

If we build triads on our major scale, we use this formula and arrive at these chords:

Chords	Imaj	IIm	IIIm	IVmaj	Vmaj	MIm	VII°
Scale Tones							
Key of C	Cmaj	Dminor	Eminor	Fmaj	Gmaj	Aminor	B°

C Scale Harmonized

To see how knowledge of harmonized scales can increase the possibilities open to you, consider the following.

Harmonizing Major Scales

Using the formula given on the preceding page for constructing chords on major scale tones, write the following harmonized scales.

Melodic Development on Harmonized Major Scales

Play the following studies by ear in all keys—Then write your own ideas and play them by ear through the cycle of keys.

Play all studies in C, F, Bb, Eb, Ab, Db, Gb, B, E, A, D, G.

The importance of playing arpeggios on harmonized scales is that it gives the player a good ear for the intervals within the scale and it gives some ideas on passing tones which create tension and those which release tension.

or - to use a leading tone

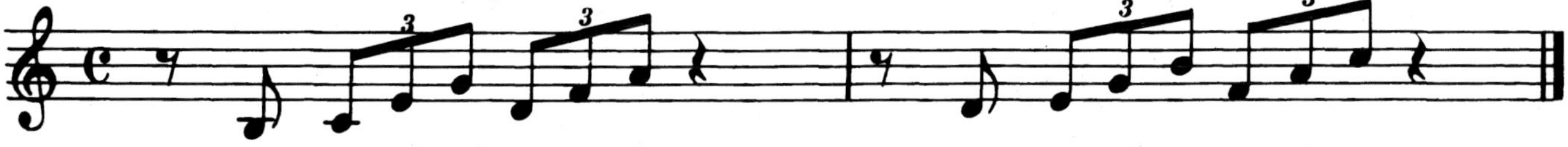

Write Your Own

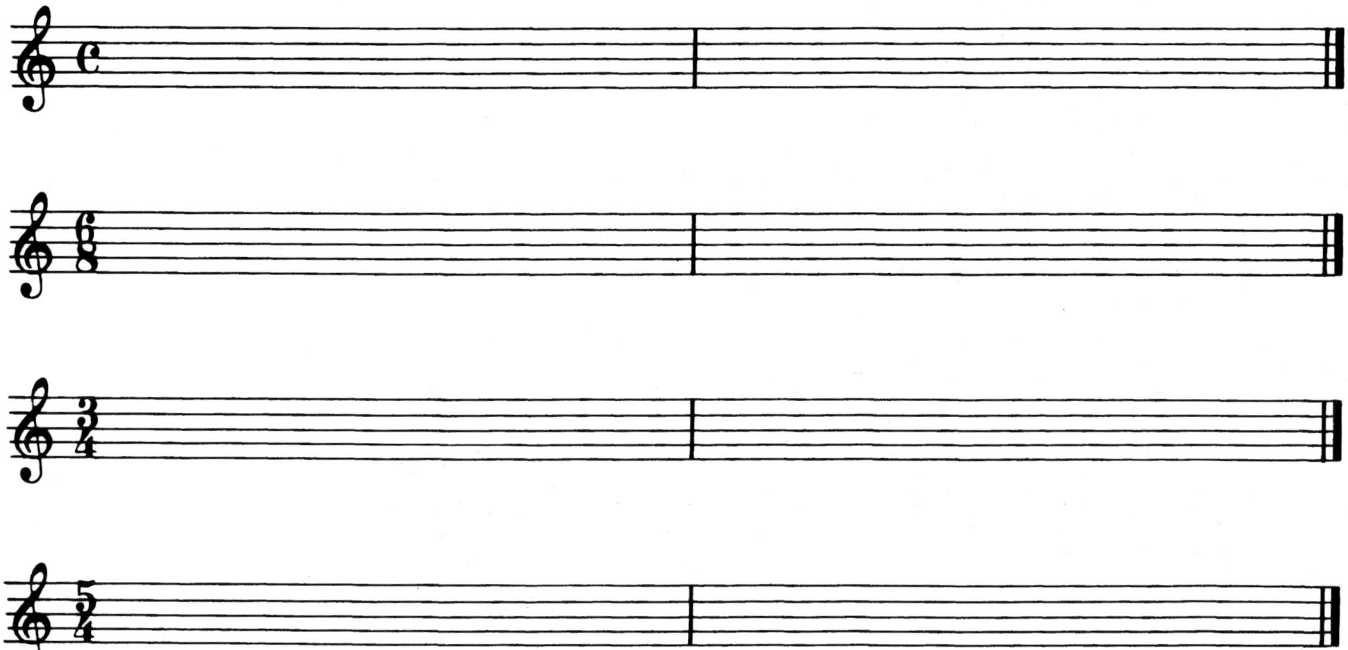

Dorian Scale Harmonized

The formula for harmonizing the dorian scale is:
Type of triad - Imin - IImin - IIImaj - Vmin - VI° - VIImaj:
Write the following harmonized scales and experiment by writing and playing your own arpeggio ideas, your ear will govern the use of certain arpeggio patterns in a given chordal situation.

Aeolian or Pure Minor Harmonized

Formula: Im - II° - IIImaj - IVmin - Vmin - VImaj - VIImaj
Write and experiment with the following harmonized scales.

C Pure minor harmonized

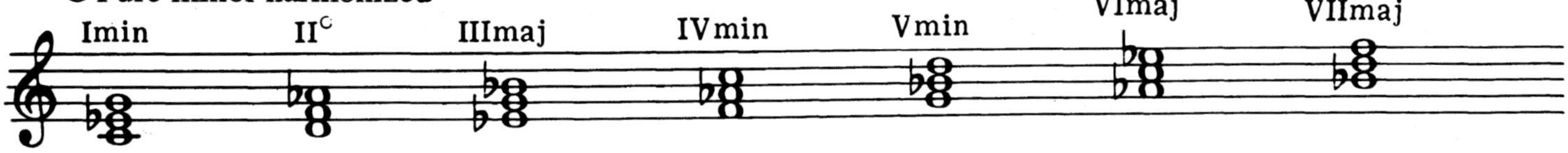

F

B♭

E♭

A♭

D♭

G♭

B

E

A

D

G

Ascending Melodic Minor Harmonized

Formula: Imin. - IImin. - IIIaug. - IVmaj. - Vmaj - VI° - VII°
Write and experiment with the following scales.

C Melodic Minor (Ascending)

Harmonic Minor Scale Harmonized

Formula: Im - II° - IIIaug. - IVmin. - Vmaj - VImaj - VII°
Write and experiment with the following scales.

C Harmonic Minor

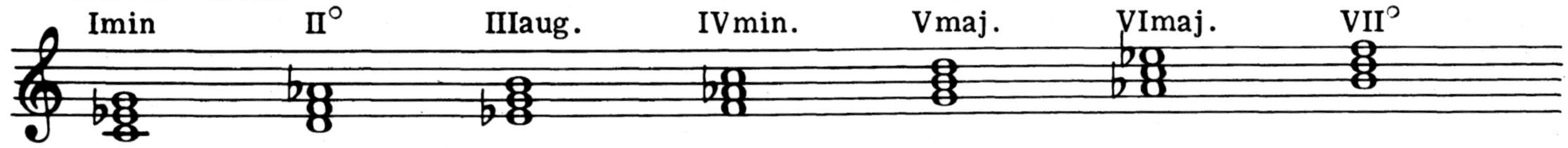

F

B♭

E♭

A♭

D♭

G♭

B

E

A

D

G

Phrygian Mode Harmonized

Formula: Imin. - IImaj. - IIImaj. - IVmin. - V° - VImaj - VIImin.
Write and experiment with the following scales.

Half Diminished Locrian Harmonized

Formula: I° - IImaj. - IIImin. - IVmin. - Vmaj. - VImaj. - VIImin.
Write and experiment with the following scales.

Mixolydian Scale Harmonized

For use against dom. 7th chords

Formula: Imaj. - IIm - III° - IVmaj - Vmin. - VImin. - VIImaj.
Write and experiment with the following scales.

C Mixolydian

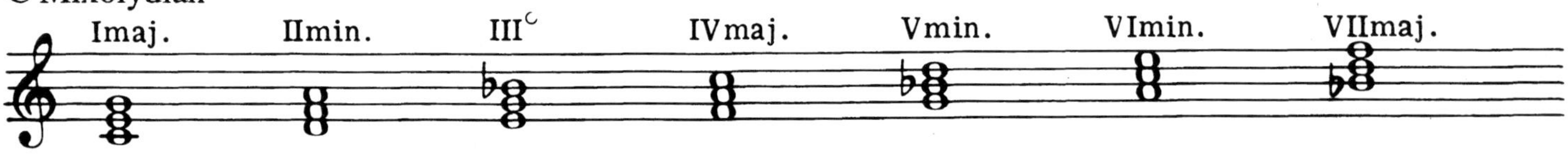

F

B♭

E♭

A♭

D♭

G♭

B

E

A

D

G